Get the job you really *want*

This is an important book.

It is outstandingly well written, and it is much needed right now. It provides a crafted plan and a toolbox of resources for job seekers and careerists alike.

I have been in the business of helping people manage their careers for several decades, and I loved this book.

The book is laid out logically and clearly, and can be read beginning to end – or dipped into according to your need.

Erin's writing is lucid and passionate but, more than that, it is based on a deep reservoir of experience in the field. Erin has helped a vast number of people with their career evolution. She does it every day. The result is a book that is erudite and informed, but also pragmatic rather than academic. That is its appeal and unique value.

I enjoyed the clear and concise advice, and the many valuable examples and anecdotes found throughout.

The real beauty of this work is how practical and accessible it is. If you are a graduate looking for your first job, you will find priceless tips as well as wise words to save you from costly errors in your job search. Equally, if you are a professional heavyweight with your career well on track and the next step looming, this book will give you an edge in a competitive market. I found myself nodding in agreement all the way through, but also loving the fact that I was learning plenty as I went along.

There is nothing important left out. I enjoyed the early chapters on goal-setting and career alignment. These alone make the book a must-read. The online branding advice is spot on, as we often see people harming their job prospects, even their careers, with poor online decisions, or lack of effort in positioning their personal brands. You might be forgiven for thinking the chapters on resume preparation and applying for a job might be a little dry. Not at all! They're so well-explained and written with such enthusiasm for the task at hand that they're fun and highly illuminating. The crucial topic of preparing for and performing at the interview gets terrific treatment, and all of us can learn from the advice here.

This book is easy to digest and packed with helpful advice, and doubles as a motivational primer.

I recommend it to anyone embarking on a job search – indeed, anyone who cares about career progression and wants to maximise their potential.

I have known and worked with Erin for a decade. She is an exceptional businesswoman and leader.

It turns out she is an outstanding author too.

Greg Savage, recruitment adviser, investor and best-selling author of *The Savage Truth* book

Recruitment Ninja! Just one of the titles shared around the corridors of the recruitment agency to which I belong. To achieve this illustrious title, you must have interviewed a minimum of 1000 job seekers. Erin Devlin long ago crossed this threshold! Erin, like many of us in the recruitment industry, is a store of anecdotes, facts and advice that are rarely shared in the written word. *Get the job you really want* is finally the resource that does just that. The 15 chapters bring together decades of recruitment, employment and business experience in a concise and easy-to-read reference. They condense lessons from thousands of CVs, reviews, interviews, negotiations and dream jobs successfully secured.

Erin brings her advice to the page with a gusto that she has displayed throughout her career in the recruitment industry and also her highly successful time within the arts. Just as she successfully climbed the ranks to the Australian Ballet with determination, hard work and collaboration, Erin has used these qualities to bring together a sharp, concise and easily understood checklist for aspirational job seekers.

As a 25-year veteran of the recruitment industry myself, I am delighted that Erin has taken the initiative, as she has done in her six years working closely with me at people2people, to build a reference for everyone engaging in the job market. Whether you are at the beginning of your career, at an unexpected turning point or at an important career junction, you can visit the following pages again and again to inform your job search and guide you along the path to accepting the job you really want.

Mark Smith, Group Managing Director, people2people Recruitment

The competition for the best jobs with the best employers has never been hotter. Finding and securing the right job at the right time, appropriate to your career ambitions, is one of the most important things you will do in your life, and you can't afford to undertake this task without expert help. *Get the job you really want* is the expert help you need in 15 easy-to-read and actionable chapters, complete with examples, checklists, templates and worksheets. Erin has extracted every last piece of her extensive and invaluable knowledge to equip ambitious job seekers with the best, most comprehensive and up-to-date resources and advice to help them secure the job that could change their career trajectory – and maybe even their whole life. This book is compulsory reading for anybody who wants more from their career and is hungry for the ultimate practical guide to help them achieve it.

Ross Clennett, high-performance recruitment coach, trainer, blogger and commentator on the Australian recruitment industry

Get the job *really* want

Erin Devlin

*For my boys Will, Alex and Tom,
and all the brilliant individuals reading this book.
Your future is bright. Let's go get it.*

First published in 2021 by Major Street Publishing Pty Ltd
E: info@majorstreet.com.au W: majorstreet.com.au M: +61 421 707 983

© Erin Devlin 2021
The moral rights of the author have been asserted.

 A catalogue record for this book is available from the National Library of Australia

Printed book ISBN: 978-0-6489803-6-0
Ebook ISBN: 978-0-6489803-7-7

All rights reserved. Except as permitted under *The Australian Copyright Act 1968* (for example, a fair dealing for the purposes of study, research, criticism or review), no part of this book may be reproduced, stored in a retrieval system, communicated or transmitted in any form or by any means without prior written permission. All inquiries should be made to the publisher.

Cover design by Simone Geary
Internal design by Production Works
Printed in Australia by Ovato, an Accredited ISO AS/NZS 14001:2004 Environmental Management System Printer.

10 9 8 7 6 5 4 3 2 1

Disclaimer: The material in this publication is in the nature of general comment only, and neither purports nor intends to be advice. Readers should not act on the basis of any matter in this publication without considering (and if appropriate taking) professional advice with due regard to their own particular circumstances. The author and publisher expressly disclaim all and any liability to any person, whether a purchaser of this publication or not, in respect of anything and the consequences of anything done or omitted to be done by any such person in reliance, whether whole or partial, upon the whole or any part of the contents of this publication.

Contents

Foreword	xi

Part I: Get ready, get set

Chapter 1: It's good to have a goal	3
Chapter 2: You are valuable	17
Chapter 3: What an employer can offer you	31

Part II: Your online profile

Chapter 4: Let's start with LinkedIn	47
Chapter 5: Build your personal brand online	57

Part III: CVs, resumes and cover letters

Chapter 6: Put together a great CV	71
Chapter 7: Make yourself stand out	89
Chapter 8: Cover letters with impact	103

Part IV: Search and apply

Chapter 9: Your job search	117
Chapter 10: Recruitment agencies	135
Chapter 11: Screening and assessment	151

Part V: Interview for success

Chapter 12: Prepare for your interview	169
Chapter 13: Interview with intent	181
Chapter 14: Manage job offers	193
Chapter 15: Set yourself up for success	205

Thank you	214
References and resources	219
Useful websites	223
About the author	227

Foreword

This book is like insider trading for job seekers – it's so good you'll feel as if you've been tipped off by the employer.

Job hunting is a fine art. In this book, Erin not only gives you the paint, she gives you the canvas, the easel, the brush strokes and even the gallery to sell your masterpiece – the masterpiece which is you!

Never before has the job market been harder to navigate than now. Economic, technological, environmental, health, business and social changes have all combined to deliver a truly complex, and occasionally demoralising, experience for job seekers regardless of age, gender, race, qualification or experience. This book is extremely timely and important, not just because it brings real world advice and insights, but because the advice is highly relevant, easy to apply and extremely generous. Erin Devlin is the recruiter you want as your agent, and now you have her.

Erin has written a guide to finding the right job that has a warmth and understanding that you won't find anywhere else, in my opinion. When you read this book, you feel as if Erin knows you and what makes you tick. She knows that life and passion can work both for and against you, and that job hunting can make you feel vulnerable and empowered, all at the same time. These are the defining features of this publication, which make it so truly valuable.

As the Chief Executive of Australia and New Zealand's industry association for the recruitment and staffing industry, I know how important it is to care for candidates during the job hunting process. It is critical that recruiters communicate in a manner that can be understood, absorbed and leveraged so that, regardless of the outcome, the candidate can learn and grow. Having known Erin for many years, it is a delight to see her articulate and generous communication style find its way onto the pages of this, her first publication. Erin will always give you time and clarity, regardless of who you are, and this book is no exception. After reading it for the first time, Erin's book actually made me want to try my hand at finding a new job, even though I love what I do. It inspires and challenges you to be better and prouder of who you are and what you can offer. Very few books on job seeking have the capacity to do that.

No matter what your next move may be, whether it be your first or twelfth permanent role, your eighty-second contract role or your first advice to your son or daughter, you will be the smartest person in the market if you take this book off the shelf and share it with those who you want to see succeed in work and life.

Charles Cameron, Vice-President of the World Employment Confederation and Chief Executive Officer of The Recruitment, Consulting & Staffing Association of Australia and New Zealand (RCSA)

Part I
Get ready, get set

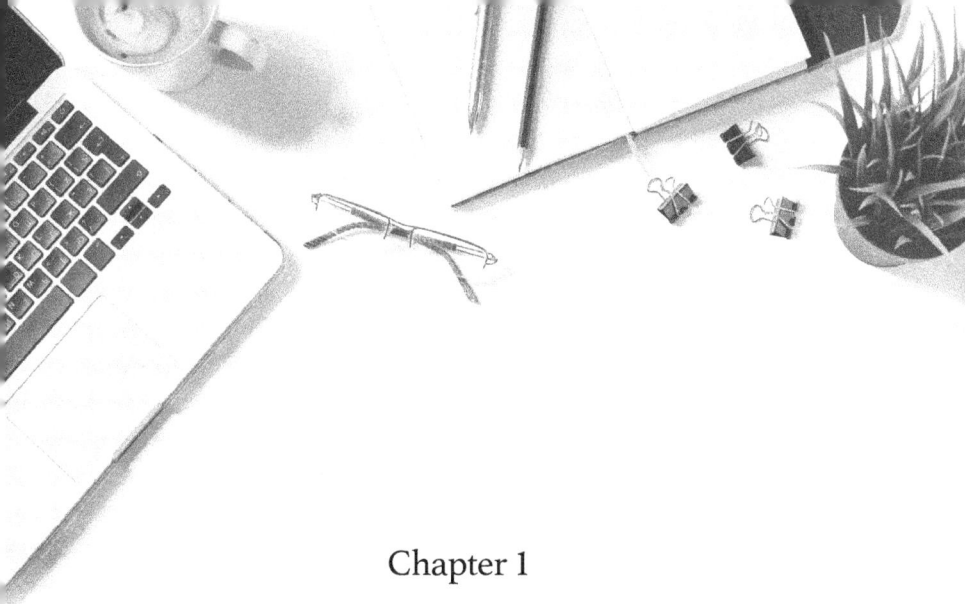

Chapter 1

It's good to have a goal

- Align your career plans with your life plans.
- Determine your career direction.
- Set S.M.A.R.T. goals to underpin your career success.

As children and young adults, we're told we can do anything in life. Our socials are peppered with catchphrases such as 'Just do it', 'Believe in yourself', and 'With hard work you can have, be or do anything'. And I love this – the positivity, the joy in it. This attitude of ambition will get you very far in life. To be truly kind to ourselves though, and to succeed in our careers, we must bring our vision into focus and break it down into bite-sized chunks that can help form the building blocks of our success.

You *can* be the owner of your own multimillion-dollar clothing business, the social worker making someone's life better, the environmentalist saving the planet, the accountant keeping order or the doctor saving lives. To get there, you'll need patience, focus and a plan.

Getting to know many successful people over the years, I've noticed that not one of them has landed where they are by accident. They often come from humble beginnings, but have set goals along the way, made intelligent career moves and taken risks. They have been deliberate, focussed and strategic. I have observed a number of common strategies and steps that they've taken, many of which I will share in this book.

Getting a job is one thing. Getting the job you *really* want is another.

This where we start – looking at you and what you want in your life and at work. Your career is only one part of this picture. If you are reading this book to gain employment, looking to advance your career or return to the workforce after a break, it's a great time to stop and reflect on what you actually want in your career and life. So let's take a look at the big picture first.

The life you want to live

Every great career is built upon a foundation of learning and a series of tiny decisions made right over a lifetime of hard work. When we think about future careers, we often think about them as being separate from our 'personal lives', but the reality is that the two intersect and influence one another more than we think. By looking at our lives holistically and understanding what it is that we want in the future as a *person*, not just as an *employee*, we set ourselves up with a great chance of bringing our work and home lives into harmony.

> ### Reflection
>
> Growing up in Melbourne, Australia, I took a liking to dance as a young girl. I loved the social element and how I could move my body, and I really enjoyed performing with my friends. Little did I know that it would lead me towards a professional career as a ballerina. Going on to dance with the Australian Ballet gave me joys that I can't even describe, but it also took my career in a direction that was different to what I had envisaged for myself.

I loved my family and my friends; I loved food, art, sport, music and getting out into the community. Suddenly, as a professional dancer, I felt out of balance and out of touch with the things that were so important to me in life. And while I had the privilege of going on stage in front of thousands of people and making them smile, I longed for more balance, flexibility and leadership in my career.

Take a step back from your own life. What do you love most about being in the world? Is it your family? Your health? Giving back to the community? Earning money? What *is* it that's important to you? Remember, you can apply for any job that you like, but if you don't know what it is that you want, you won't love what it is that you do.

What if you *don't* know yet? What if you aren't sure?

Reflection

I had no idea that I would eventually end up running a recruitment business, or that I would absolutely love it. I didn't know that I would travel the world as cabin crew in my twenties and see some of the most spectacular places on earth, but I did, and I loved it.

You don't have to know *exactly* what it is that you want to be or what you want to do, but one thing is for sure: be clear about *what is important to you in life*. This will play into your career. It will play into your job search and it will ultimately influence your happiness and success.

Success – and how you define it – depends on who you ask, and when. To one person, success is becoming a waiter in a five-star resort in a beautiful part of the world; to another it's working close to home to spend more time with family, and to another it's building a name for themselves in business. All are successful in their own way and in their own time.

Let's explore further what career success means to you. You can use the 'life and career vision board' and 'vision statement' exercises over the page to get you started.

✍ LIFE AND CAREER VISION BOARD

Using an art board, the space here, or a platform like Pinterest, you can pull together images that resonate with you relating to your life and career, or write some descriptive text. Examples might include a businessperson winning an award, a mother holding a baby, a traveller on top of a mountain or a social worker reaching out to someone in need. Choose images and words that resonate with you.

✍ VISION STATEMENT

Create a vision statement for yourself which reflects you and what you want your career to look like in five or ten years' time; e.g. 'To be a world-class solar panels expert, furthering the use of renewable energy'.

_____

_____

_____

_____

Interests

To love what you do, look for jobs that will align closely with your interests. Think about how you spend your time and what you enjoy doing. Do you love working with your hands? Creating order? Socialising? Achieving goals? Whatever it is that really interests you, ensure that it is present in jobs that you are considering. Take some time now to list your key interests below:

📝 INTERESTS

What do you love doing? How do you spend your spare time?

_____

_____

_____

Motivating factors

When we are considering a job, we are likely to be driven by motivating factors that encourage us to say yes. By compiling the list below, you can clarify what it is that is important to you in a job, incorporating some of your interests and lifestyle preferences.

📝 MOTIVATING FACTORS

From the list of motivating factors below and on the next page, circle those which are important to you, or list additional options. Choose your top ten and rank them in order of importance. Keep them handy when assessing job opportunities to help you choose a job that you'll enjoy.

- Caring for the environment
- Social good
- Giving back
- Community engagement
- Making money
- Status
- Business ownership
- Entrepreneurship
- Leadership opportunities
- Making people happy
- Having order and structure
- Being creative

- Lots of social interaction
- Meaningful work
- Being rewarded or recognised
- Standard hours
- Flexibility
- Work-life balance
- Being seen as an expert
- Close to home
- International travel
- Autonomy
- Work friendships
- Growth and development
- Being innovative
- Career progression
- Working with technology
- Ability to challenge
- Problem solving
- Realising potential
- Great work environment
- Stimulating work
- Being physically active
- Other?

1. _____
2. _____
3. _____
4. _____
5. _____
6. _____
7. _____
8. _____
9. _____
10. _____

Strengths

Even if singing in the shower is one of your interests, it may not be something that an employer is willing to pay you to do (harsh but true). Being honest with yourself about what your strengths are and what you're good at can help align you with jobs that suit your natural abilities. List your top three to five strengths opposite and keep them front of mind as you assess jobs. Working in a job that utilises these strengths will be less strenuous and more enjoyable, and will lead to better outcomes for you and your employer.

STRENGTHS
What are you good at? What are your natural abilities?

_____

_____

_____

_____

_____

Career direction

Even if you're clear on your career direction and profession, it still pays to develop your values, understand your motivations and set career goals. For those who are still at the point of exploring professions, the key to selecting a job you love is to align it with your interests, motivations, values and goals. As you move through the next couple of chapters, assess each of these elements against potential jobs and professions. You'll want to take yourself through a process of self-assessment using the exercises I've provided, career exploration and career identification, and then make a plan.

'I just don't know what's out there' is the comment I hear most when working with professional athletes who are transitioning from a career in sport to a new job. Fortunately, there are many great ways to explore potential professions and jobs. First, I suggest they take some time to look up different jobs online and understand the purpose of each, what the main tasks and duties are, and what the work environment is like. They can then match these up to their job motivations, their life and career vision board, and the values that we will go on to explore in Chapter 2. I also encourage them to take a career assessment test (CAT) to get some ideas. CATs can assess a person's personality, interests and motivations, and suggest jobs to explore further.

You may not be a former elite athlete, but these are good places to start.

Talk with people who work in the areas you have an interest in. Perhaps you have a family member or friend who knows someone in the area of work you are considering? If not, you can reach out directly to people in the field to explore further. Work experience, shadowing, internships, charity volunteering and temp and contract work can also be great ways to get a feel for a new work environment and job before committing to further study or work options.

If you would like to explore professions and potential jobs further, you can also meet with a career counsellor or practitioner. They can guide you towards some pathways to explore and answer many of your questions. Your local career development association may have a list of practitioners which you can look up. I have put together a list of online resources that you can access to explore your career direction, which you can find in the 'Useful websites' section at the back of this book.

Changing careers

It's okay not to be linear. The U.S. Department of Labor has reported that the average person will change jobs 12 times during their working life. Often this can include a career change or two. Whether it's learning something new, earning more, giving back or achieving particular goals, there are many reasons for a career change. This is something I can relate to closely, for I could never have imagined the career changes I have experienced in my life till now.

Reflection

I accepted my first contract with the Australian Ballet at the age of 12. Walking out on stage in their production of *Swan Lake* was like a dream come true. Over seven years, I danced professionally in productions such as *Romeo and Juliet*, *Études*, *The Nutcracker*, *The Sleeping Beauty*, *Don Quixote* and a range of contemporary triple bills.

Leaving this behind, it was time to explore the world as I embraced my new job as cabin crew for Emirates airline. Living in the Middle East and working with crew from over 130 different countries was an amazing way to open up my mind to new cultures and experiences. I learnt about teamwork, quality and great customer service. And although I thought that I had left my previous career behind, it was an old ballet injury – recurring stress fractures – that brought my jet setting life to a close. I had pushed my body to the limit for so long, it was time to finally treat it kindly.

Landing back in Australia, I registered with a recruitment agency for temp opportunities and they offered me a job with their own agency directly. It was the start of a career that I love. Since then, I've built and merged businesses, grown and developed teams, completed a post-graduate qualification, and had the privilege of working with hundreds of savvy and intelligent job seekers and employers. They have taught me a huge amount about life, business and what's important.

I can think of an accomplished, award-winning television producer who has now gone on to become a hospital-based physiotherapist, helping people recover from trauma and return to what they love doing; a documentary producer who worked in disability services and is now a teacher helping students to flourish; and an international singer who supported artists like John Farnham, Julio Iglesias, Tim Rice and Tina Turner, who went on to charity work, coordinating fundraising efforts and helping people in the community. There are many more examples of people who have undertaken a career change – maybe you're considering one yourself.

Utilise the career direction exercises in the previous section to explore different professions and understand what will be involved if you do make the change. Later in this book, we'll look at how you can get your foot in the door if you decide to take a new career direction and how to market yourself effectively to employers. It takes courage, focus and determination to change careers, but the results can be incredibly rewarding.

Setting career goals

When assessing what it is that you really want from your career and job, it's helpful to break it down into specific goals, such as becoming an expert in your field, owning your own business or mastering a particular skill. These goals underpin your career plan and are important to establish before you start applying for jobs.

Research profiles of people who you admire. Examples might be a scientist who is conducting world-leading health research, a florist brightening people's days or a marketing consultant involved in lots of creative projects. Whatever it is, don't just think of the *idea* of it – actually find some real-life people who you want to emulate or draw inspiration from. Of course, you'll forge your own journey, but having people in sight that make you want to take action can help create focus and shape your career goals.

Use a formula, like George T. Doran's S.M.A.R.T. goal acronym, that can give you a clear vision to work towards. S.M.A.R.T. stands for Specific, Measurable, Assignable, Realistic and Time-based. For example, you might say:

> 'I'd like to be an expert in the field of ski instructing and be
> hired by one of the world's top five resorts in the next six years.'

Or:

> 'I'd like to own a business that solves a key social problem in
> the community in the next ten years.'

Or:

> 'I'd like to be a respected accountant, in a mid-tier firm,
> close to home, where I can spend quality time with my family,
> in five years' time.'

These are all great examples of career goals. You may have just one overarching goal or several that you'd like to explore. Remember that goals can be malleable and may change over time as your needs, wants and desires change. Initially, making money might seem like the most important thing to you; but later, giving back or championing diversity initiatives may become more important.

You can make micro-goals too, like 'Learn how to use Adobe InDesign to an advanced level within the next year' or 'Attain my Six Sigma Black Belt in the next three years'.

CAREER GOALS
What are your short- and long-term career goals?

1. _____

2. _____

3. _____

4. _____

5. _____

Take action

For each career goal that you've set, think about what you need to do to achieve each goal. Is there some training or a university course that you need to complete? Are you required to obtain a particular certificate or qualification? Are there areas of interest that you'd like to explore further through research, conversations or work experience? Decide what action steps are needed to propel you towards achieving your career goals. Work out a timeframe, as well as practical and logistical steps to undertake each action.

📝 **ACTION ITEMS**

What action steps do you need to take to achieve your career goals?

1. _____

2. _____

3. _____

4. _____

5. _____

Make a career plan

> *'A goal without a plan is just a wish.'*
>
> ~ Antoine de Saint-Exupéry

As you move through this book, you can start to form your career plan and strategy. You may not realise it, but you've already taken many of the steps in this chapter that you need to make this happen. If you are still in the career exploration phase, then your plan may include the top three professions or jobs you are interested in exploring and what steps you will take to assess them further. If you know what your chosen profession or job is, then your plan will focus on the steps you need to take to obtain it.

Update your plan as you gather more information and move through this book from start to finish. Use the headings and template below, or take your career plan online to make it a living, breathing document. From the earlier exercises in this chapter, add in your life and career vision board, and your top motivations, interests, strengths and career goals. In Chapter 2 we'll assess values, which you can also add into your plan. As we explore different topics, from online branding to CV preparation to interview techniques, add in the practical steps you will need to take to achieve your career goals. Knowing what it is that you want for your own life can help give you a laser-like focus for your career. Better still, making a plan to help you get there can put your success in motion.

CAREER PLAN

Vision
- Life and career vision board
- Vision statement for five or ten years' time

Interests, motivations, strengths and values
- What's important to you in a job?
- What are your interests?
- What are you good at?
- What are your values?

Profession
- Chosen profession, or jobs and professions to explore

Goals
- S.M.A.R.T. goals that underpin your career vision

Action
- Action steps you need to take to achieve your career goals
- Include education, training, work experience and exploration steps
- Include skills, knowledge and certifications you need

Status
- Include status updates as you take steps towards your career goals

 *If you would like to access a free career plan template, scan the QR code here, or visit people2people.com.au.*

☕ Coffee break

Before applying for jobs, decide what is important to you by developing a life and career vision, and understanding your interests, motivating factors, strengths, values and career direction. Explore jobs, or deepen your knowledge of the profession you have already chosen. Set some S.M.A.R.T. goals and make a career plan. Putting this into action can set you up for success. Most importantly, keep your goals handy as you start to consider jobs. Ensuring that your career plan, goals and action steps are aligned with possible opportunities can help bring you closer to working in a job that you love.

Now that you've given some thought to where your job search will ultimately lead you, and you're starting to visualise what your future will look like, let's take a closer look at you. In the next chapter, you can explore why you are valuable and why an employer should offer you the job that you *really* want.

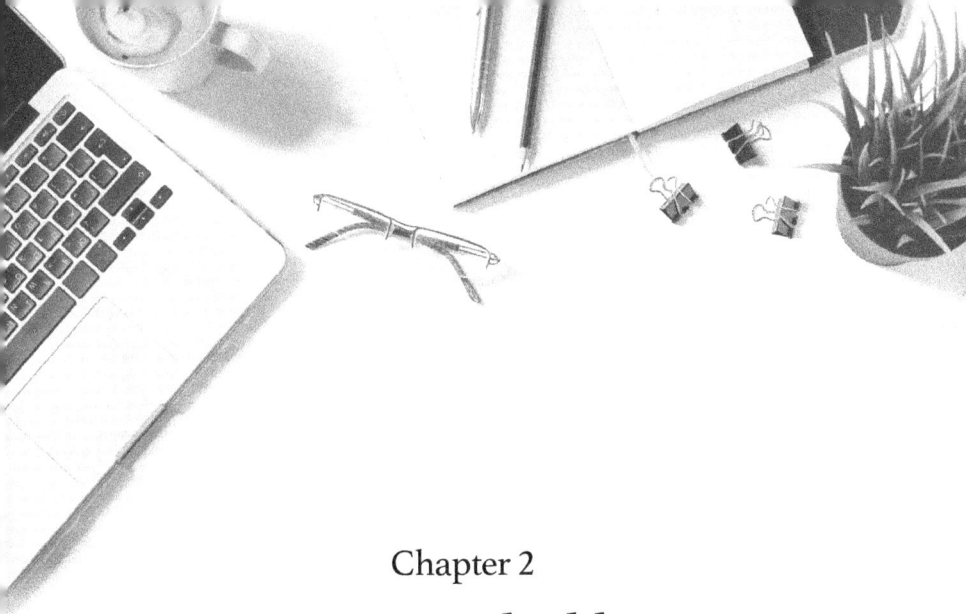

Chapter 2

You are valuable

- Develop your Employee Value Proposition.
- Articulate, qualify and quantify your achievements.
- Clarify your vision and ideas of success in your next job.

> 'Whether you think you can,
> or you think you can't, you're right.'
>
> ~ Henry Ford

Securing the job that you *really* want is all about selling yourself well to an employer. To do that, you'll need to know what's great about you: your strengths, your values, your achievements, your ideas and why you'd be a valuable member of the right team.

You might have heard of an Employer Value Proposition. It is a combination of benefits and rewards that an employer offers in exchange for your skills, experience and hard work. (We'll look at this more in Chapter 3.) But what about *your* value proposition – an *Employee*

Value Proposition (EVP)? Your EVP is what *you* can offer the company, and it's what makes you stand out.

Your EVP forms the basis of your resume or CV (curriculum vitae) and how you represent yourself at interview. It articulates your points of difference, makes you more appealing than other candidates and is ultimately what can get you the job.

Think of your EVP as a pyramid, with each layer forming an important foundation for the next, culminating in your vision for success in your job.

Employee Value Proposition

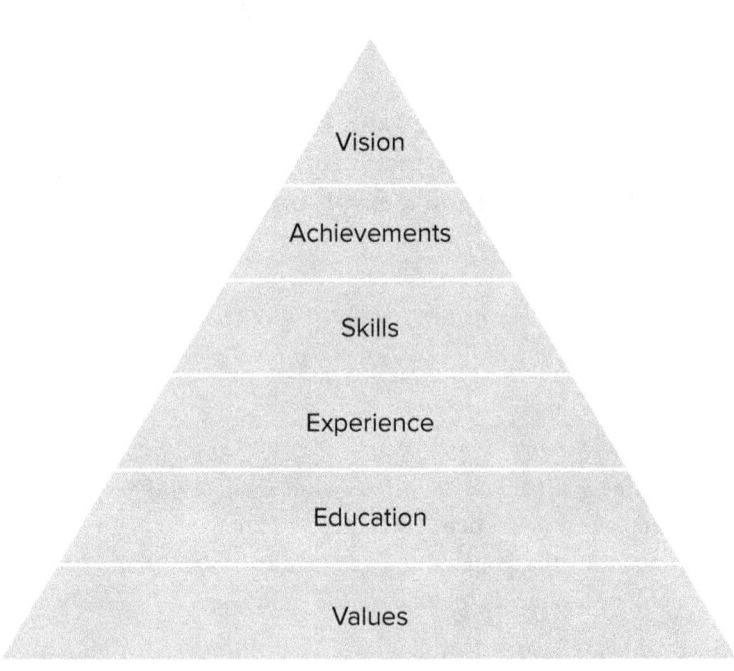

To develop your EVP further, let's start with your values.

Determining your values

Your values are what underpin your EVP. They are at the base of the pyramid because they are the foundation of success in your career. A great way to determine them is to look to people you admire and note the qualities you like about them. Maybe they have qualities that you want to emulate in your own life. You can also think of a time when you stood up for something. Why did you stand up for that cause and how does that play into your value set? Lastly, think of a time when you really *felt like you*. What were you doing at the time and how might this be reflected in your values?

✎ VALUES

Using the list overleaf, choose 20 values that really resonate with you. Then group them together under five or six related headings with an accompanying phrase. For example, you might choose values like *adventure*, *fun*, *joy*, *playfulness* and *happiness*, and therefore your key heading and phrase might be 'Happiness: having fun and seeing the positive side of situations'.

Once you've completed this exercise you will hopefully have a list of five or six core values. Here is an example of what this might look like:

- **Giving:** giving back and contributing for good
- **Happiness:** enjoying life and work, and always seeing the positive
- **Achievement:** learning, developing, seizing opportunities and continuously improving
- **Integrity:** staying true to what I believe in, and having the courage to advocate
- **Teamwork:** helping and supporting others

VALUES

Accountability	Family	Perfection
Achievement	Flexibility	Performance
Adventure	Freedom	Playfulness
Advocacy	Friendships	Popularity
Ambition	Fun	Power
Autonomy	Generosity	Proactivity
Balance	Growth	Professionalism
Brilliance	Happiness	Quality
Calmness	Health	Recognition
Career focus	Honesty	Relationships
Caring	Hope	Reliability
Challenge	Humility	Resilience
Charity	Humour	Resourcefulness
Cheerfulness	Inclusiveness	Responsibility
Cleverness	Independence	Responsiveness
Collaboration	Individuality	Risk-taking
Commitment	Innovation	Safety
Community	Inspiration	Security
Compassion	Intelligence	Self-control
Consistency	Joy	Selflessness
Contribution	Kindness	Service
Creativity	Knowledge	Simplicity
Credibility	Leadership	Spirituality
Curiosity	Learning	Stability
Decisiveness	Love	Success
Dependability	Loyalty	Teamwork
Development	Making a difference	Thoughtfulness
Diversity	Mindfulness	Trustworthiness
Empathy	Motivation	Understanding
Encouragement	Open-mindedness	Usefulness
Enthusiasm	Optimism	Versatility
Ethics	Originality	Vision
Excellence	Passion	Wealth
Fairness	Peace	Wisdom

List your values here and add them to your career plan.

_____
_____
_____
_____
_____

Your education: what counts?

The next level of your EVP pyramid is education you have completed. You can include high school, university degrees, TAFE courses, on-the-job training, online nanodegrees, short courses, mentoring programs, conferences, industry certifications and any other professional development that you have undertaken. Focus on and emphasise education that is closely aligned to the positions that you are considering. For example, you might have undertaken a barista course, but now that you're applying for a marketing assistant position, you'll want to highlight your communications degree. What qualifications you include in your CV and online profile depend on the level of education you have achieved. For example, if you are applying for a job straight out of school, you can include your high school qualifications, even listing the subjects. However, if you have a PhD, you might start with your undergraduate studies.

University degrees can show that you have a high-level strategic understanding of particular subjects and have completed detailed investigation too. A nanodegree is typically a course of study that you can complete in under 12 months and is delivered online. Completing a nanodegree or TAFE course can reflect attainment of specific job-ready skills, such as UX design, carpentry or data engineering. Mentoring and on-the-job training can also help advance your career in your current job. You can attend conferences or industry events to help reinvigorate, reshape and re-energise your thinking. We'll talk more about how to include education in your CV and online profile later. For now, note the key education that you offer as part of your EVP.

✏️ EDUCATION AND PROFESSIONAL DEVELOPMENT

_____

_____

_____

_____

_____

_____

What experience have you had?

Paid work is important in developing your career and experience in a variety of settings, but internships, volunteering and extracurricular activities are all valuable experiences too. Employers love to hear about charities you're involved in, clubs or groups that you're committed to and where you've contributed to side businesses. This type of experience gives extra insight into a candidate, because it can often demonstrate values, proactivity, leadership, work ethic, interpersonal skills and community spirit. Employers want to know what ideas you've come up with, initiatives you've sparked, projects you've driven and work you've completed. They'll be interested in the scope, size, process, outcomes and results that you've achieved. They may ask you about your mentors and your experience working with them, and who you might have led and developed yourself. Your experience may include blogs that you have written, cars or boats that you've restored or social media pages that you've managed. It depends on the job that you're pitching for, but more often than not you'll have much more experience than you think you have. Get a head start on your EVP and note some of your key experience.

📝 EXPERIENCE

_____
_____
_____
_____
_____
_____
_____
_____

What are your skills?

Having worked with more than 500 professional athletes on career planning and transition, I am always pleased to see how many of their sporting skills are transferable into new professions. However, the number of times I've heard an athlete say 'I don't have any relevant skills' is astonishing. Highly trained professional athletes have learnt to work to schedules, push their minds and bodies to the limit, contribute to teams and show leadership on and off the field. As Justine Whipper, General Manager – Player Development and Wellbeing at the Australian Cricketers' Association, explains:

> *When athletes transition from sport to another career, they often find the most challenging aspect to be understanding their worth outside of the game (industry). But by building their level of self-awareness, industry exploration, formal or informal education, work experience and networking, they develop confidence in their unique strengths and realise they are often sought after by employers.*

Whether you're straight out of university, taking the next career step or changing direction, the chances are that you have more skills than you give yourself credit for too.

Here are some examples of relevant skills that any employer would love a candidate to have. Most students will have already developed these during their studies, and professionals in their work.

Teamwork	Collaboration
Leadership	Initiative
Report writing	Entrepreneurial skills
Generating innovative ideas	Public speaking
Research skills	Presentation development
Critical thinking	Creativity
Problem solving	Interpersonal communication
Flexibility and adaptability	Technology management

Now's the time to think about your own skill set and what you've learnt at work, school, university, or from extracurricular activities like sport or charity work. Make sure you give yourself credit for all of the brilliant skills that you have obtained throughout your employment and life and articulate these well to an employer.

> **Case study**
>
> Joseph was an accountant who had listed his degree and CPA qualification on his CV. While he was a solid candidate for the position that he had applied for, the client nearly passed up his application because there was nothing that really made him stand out from other candidates. Luckily for Joseph, the employer did invite him in for an interview and was surprised to learn that he was also captain of his local cricket team. In this position he had shown leadership, collaboration, teamwork, innovation and problem solving, and these were exactly the skills that the employer was looking for. Although the accounting degree was important, hundreds of candidates who had applied had this qualification. It was the skills and experience that Joseph brought to the table from his extracurricular activities that got him the job.

You can list your key skills here and continue to develop your EVP.

KEY SKILLS

_____

_____

_____

What have you achieved?

Moving up the pyramid, let's look at your achievements. When interviewing for a job, it won't be enough to have relevant skills and experience and an interest in the position: you need to find ways to stand out. Therefore, it's critical that you showcase your achievements from earlier workplaces, not just that you *attended* work. Often recruiters see on people's CVs their positions and duties listed, but nothing about their achievements. They don't just want to know that you were in an outbound sales position for two years – they want to know whether you were *good* at it or not. Did you hit your targets consistently? Did you contribute new ideas? Were you reliable, turning up on time? Did you operate ethically and with empathy? These are the things that they want to know.

But how do you articulate that in a CV or during an interview? The first step is to think about all of the achievements that you have amassed in your career to date. If your career has been short, or you haven't had a job yet, then you might want to include achievements from school, university, sport or extracurricular activities. Here are two examples of achievements that you could list on your CV and online profile, or discuss at interview:

> 'As the Nurse Unit Manager for the Wellness Hospital, I designed and implemented a revamped infection control training module which was delivered to all incoming team members upon arrival. This led to a 30% decrease in infectious outbreaks in the unit over a 12-month period and was subsequently rolled out across the entire hospital.'

Or:

> 'When I joined Terry's Trucks as a logistics coordinator, the business was scheduling 30 trucks daily, but only able to deliver 45 loads of goods. In reviewing the driver routes and geography, and rearranging the pick-up and drop-off schedule, we were able to deliver 50 loads of goods per day, increasing our daily delivery output by 10%.'

Often when you think of achievements, you think of awards or formal accolades, but there are plenty of other forms of achievement, including:

- ideas you have contributed which have improved culture, performance or efficiency
- ways that you have given back to the community, helped to reduce environmental impact or improved diversity within a business
- key performance indicators (KPIs) that you have achieved or exceeded, such as sales results
- ways in which you have demonstrated the business's core values
- your efforts in helping colleagues
- projects you have managed successfully
- presentations you have delivered well
- problems you have solved with great outcomes
- showing proactivity that improved a situation
- achieving better return on investment (ROI)
- recognising and acting on business-critical trends
- demonstrating attention to detail that has had an impact
- showing empathy in interactions leading to a great outcome
- using influencing skills effectively
- meeting and exceeding expectations
- mentoring or developing someone to great success.

The *Collins English Dictionary* defines achievement as 'something which someone has succeeded in doing, especially after a lot of effort'. It's not about what you *did* in the job. It's what you *achieved*. After all, an employer wants to know that you will add value to their organisation.

In my experience, when I have worked with individuals to flesh out their achievements, I've found that most people underestimate themselves and what they have achieved. They often dismiss results or actions as ordinary, when in fact they are *extraordinary*. So, if you're sitting there thinking, 'This is all well and good, but I haven't done anything special', you probably have. You are likely to be more accomplished, more spectacular and more valuable than you think.

Here are some useful questions to ask yourself. Have you ever:

- been the leader in a situation? What happened? How did the group perform?
- offered up an idea that was taken on board and improved the situation?
- helped someone?
- hit a KPI?
- been given positive feedback?
- stood up for something that you believe in and made a difference?
- proactively solved a problem that no-one else had noticed?
- improved revenue, finances or return on investment (ROI)?
- made a business or environment better because of your actions?
- improved the customer experience?
- made a great website, presentation, document, or piece of work?
- noticed and flagged something that was important?

If you answered yes to any of the questions above, you definitely have achievements that you should be proud of. Take some time to list a few on the next page.

KEY ACHIEVEMENTS

_____

_____

_____

_____

_____

_____

_____

What vision and ideas do you bring to the table?

The last part of your EVP focuses on the future, and what you are going to do for the organisation and team that you'll be working in. Your ideas are typically grounded by your values. Your vision might centre around what you want to achieve in the role, but also, importantly, what you believe the organisation wants and why you think they'll hire you.

Reflection

Recently a candidate who I had referred for a National Sales Manager position was approaching his first interview. I offered him advice to create a six- and twelve-month strategy ahead of the interview, covering what he would do in the role in the short to medium term if appointed. He not only took this on board but came back prior to the interview to run me through the on-screen presentation that he had prepared. He delivered this to great success in the first interview. For the second interview he developed a tactical strategy about how he would launch and roll out the proposed product in the market, if the company were to hire him. This included a competitor analysis, prospect list, sales approach, marketing collateral requirements and timelines. The potential employer was blown away by his maturity, forward-thinking approach and deep level of understanding of the market. He'd taken the time to research, plan and prepare a strategy that would set the business up for success. While he had less management experience than several of the other shortlisted candidates, it was the way that he articulated his ideas and vision throughout the interview process that ultimately secured him the job.

Think about the job you are targeting. What would you want to achieve in the first six to twelve months of being in the role? Jot some of your ideas down below.

✍ VISION AND IDEAS

_____
_____
_____
_____
_____
_____
_____
_____

☕ **Coffee break**

Your EVP is the starting point for your CV, online profile and what you want to discuss in an interview setting. Develop it through understanding your values, education, experience, skills and achievements. Finally, show an employer what it is that you would like to achieve in the job if you were appointed. Having your EVP clear in your mind can help you secure the job that you *really* want. But first, let's explore what an employer can offer you.

Chapter 3

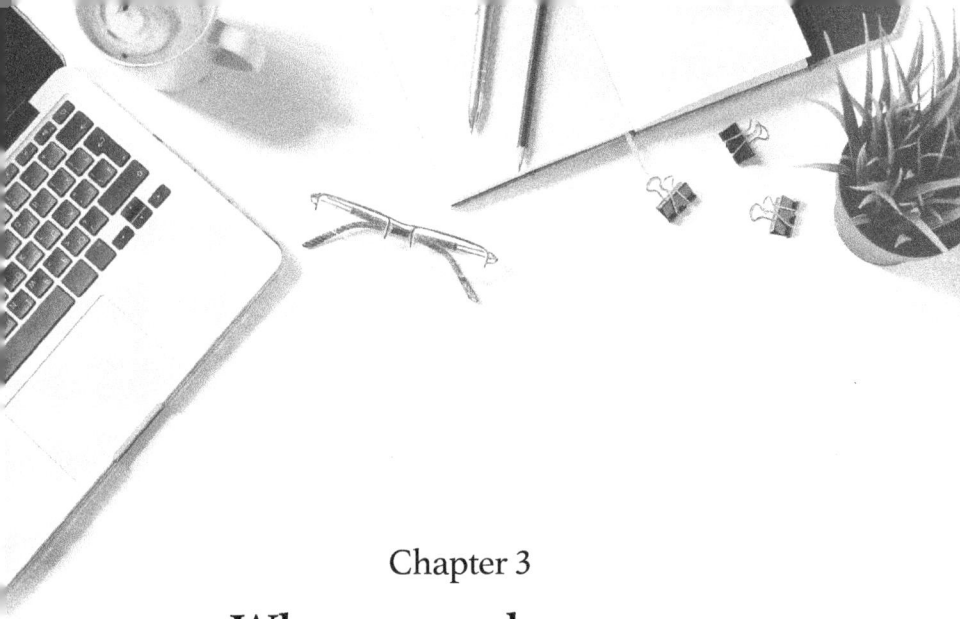

What an employer can offer you

- Explore Employer Value Propositions and what's on offer.
- Understand employment options and types of work.
- Ensure fair pay and conditions.

The recruitment process is a two-way street. The employer might be assessing you for a job in their company, but it's also your opportunity to assess them. You've worked hard to get to where you are, and you're not about to throw that away for just *any old job*. Taking the next step is a big decision, and it's one that can set you up well for the next five years and beyond. Gallup's 2017 *State of the American Workplace* report found that only 33% of employees are engaged at work, while in the world's best companies the engagement level was over 70%. Being engaged at work is key to being happy at work. Aligning your values, goals, strengths, personality and preferences with the right organisation can help you get there. In this chapter let's consider what an employer can offer you.

Employer Value Proposition

The EVP we look at in this chapter is an *Employer* Value Proposition. It's the way that employers can stand out and be attractive to you as a job seeker, and how they can retain you over the long term.

An EVP is only useful if it is actually lived within the organisation. You can get a sense of this by how the organisation promotes itself. Be wary of viewing just one shiny marketing video that's been put together specifically for the organisation's EVP. Instead, you can explore a range of resources, such as:

- company social media pages
- job advertisements
- website and career pages
- reviews
- annual reports
- conversations with current and previous employees
- conversations with customers
- news coverage
- industry publications
- job boards.

Remember that there are always two sides to every story. If you're reading online reviews or news articles with a particular view, ensure that you check out other sources too, to get a balanced understanding.

The best organisations that I've worked with have an EVP that is truly lived and breathed and is part of their DNA. They see their employees as individuals, with lives outside of work, with passions, interests, opinions and great value to add. They play to people's strengths, focus on the wins and celebrate successes. They communicate clearly and often, and with great transparency. They are strategic in their approach, collaborative in their design and inclusive in their environments. They foster high-performance cultures through loyalty, empowerment and recognition.

Some of the more tangible benefits that organisations might offer as part of their EVP include:

- flexible working
- wellness programs
- employee assistance programs
- discounted gym memberships
- income/life insurance
- increased superannuation contributions
- commission/bonus structure
- unlimited/purchased leave
- additional paid parental leave
- professional development
- study reimbursement
- career planning
- international travel/transfers
- internal promotions and career path
- finance discounts
- car leasing or salary packaging
- provided meals/snacks
- coffee machine or in-house bar
- profit share options
- games/novelties, e.g. pool table or slide.

While the above benefits are amazing and help make a great work environment, research tells us that other factors are just as important, if not more so. These can include whether your manager provides you with autonomy, how your values align with the organisation's values and whether you feel appreciated. We also know that companies that are ethnically diverse are 35% more likely to have above-average financial performance and richer ideas and perspectives.

Values alignment is key in selecting an employer, so it leads the list of areas to ask about before taking that leap. Here are my top ten must-have areas to assess when deciding on an employer:

1. **Values alignment:** Do you feel that your own values are aligned with those of the organisation?
2. **Culture:** Are you going to enjoy working in their environment? Are they collaborative? Inclusive? Team-oriented? How do they celebrate success? How do they value their team members?
3. **Benefits:** What remuneration and benefits package do they offer? Do they pay the market rate? Do they offer additional perks?
4. **Meaningful work:** Will your work at this company do something good for the environment, community, innovation or for other people?
5. **Career progression:** What future career opportunities are available within this business, and what can this job do to develop your career?
6. **Training and development:** Does the company have a formal training and development program? Do they have regular feedback opportunities and performance reviews?
7. **Flexibility and work-life balance:** Does the organisation manage by outcomes, not hours? Do they value employee contribution through results and other actions? Do they provide flexible working options with hours, leave, hot-desking and/or working from home?
8. **Location:** Where is the business located and what does it give you access to during your lunchbreaks or after work? Is it close to home, cafes, shops or other businesses?
9. **Environment:** What is the physical workspace like? Is it light, bright and environmentally friendly? Are there lunch facilities and/or breakout areas that you might enjoy?
10. **Performance:** How has the business been performing and what do its future prospects look like?

Take some time to assess employers thoroughly before making that application or accepting a job. You'll find out a lot about the business during the interview process and will want to make the right decision. Choosing well is that 'sliding door' moment in time when your life and career will change forever.

> **Reflection**
>
> When I put my recruitment business out to market, I had several interested parties. Each of these I assessed and considered not primarily based on the financial consideration they were putting forward, but on the alignment of my values to theirs. Essentially, I would be working there. Yes, as an owner, but also an employee, running the Victorian branch of our newly merged company. And it was important to me that I would enjoy it, and that the work would satisfy what I needed and desired from an employer. What drew me to the company that I ultimately chose to merge with? It was the people, the culture, the values alignment, the innovation and the forward-thinking attitude of the company's executives. I could see that the leaders within the business were people who celebrated success. They worked very hard but seemed to be having a whole lot of fun along the way! It didn't look to be a dull place, people2people, but somewhere I could grow, celebrate, have a great career and make a difference.

So, what will *you* look for in an employer? Will it be their fancy coffee machine and ball pit in the corner of the breakout area? Will it be the remuneration and financial benefits that get you over the line? Or will it be their contribution to the community and doing good in their wake? You decide. It's your career.

What are the various types of employment?

Before you start your search for employment, consider which type of work suits you best. Most job seekers focus on finding permanent employment, but there are actually a lot of other options available that can have huge career benefits. They can be a good stepping stone into full-time work but are also beneficial in their own right. Following are the various types of employment and the pros and cons of each.

Permanent employment

The greatest benefit of permanent work tends to be the level of security you can enjoy, knowing that your employment isn't due to finish on a set date. You can build your career goals at the company, knowing what career paths are available and what you need to do to progress. You can assess company culture, benefits and reputation before joining, and can often benefit from strong training and development investment from your employer. Permanent work won't protect you from redundancies, but by assessing the company's performance, reputation and future prospects, you can make an informed decision.

Temporary employment

Temporary employment is where you are engaged by a company on a specific project, to help manage heavier workflow, to cover various forms of leave or to support other business requirements. You may be given an indication of the duration of the assignment but not likely a definite end date. Companies often engage temporary employees when they need flexibility in their workforce, and when they need to scale up or down quickly.

> **Reflection**
>
> As a result of COVID-19, many businesses needed to quickly hire customer service representatives to manage a huge influx of new calls. The uncertainty that COVID-19 created and the questions that it raised meant that many businesses had to be available to answer additional questions from customers. Many of these positions were hired on a temporary basis to allow for an increase in workload during COVID-19 and a reduction in employee numbers once the surge in customer demand had passed. Examples of these businesses include online food delivery, banks, government departments, rental companies, airlines and travel businesses.

You can be engaged in temporary employment on a casual or contract basis. You might be employed directly by the company at which you're working or via a recruitment agency, or you might even be self-employed.

On-hire casual, temporary or contract employment

'On-hire work' is the term used for work completed at a host site via a recruitment agency. Often this is referred to as 'labour hire' within skilled labour trade and industrial environments, 'agency work' in healthcare environments, or 'temp or contract work' within office-based environments. In this arrangement, the agency becomes your employer and can offer you a variety of assignments in your area of expertise. As you complete assignments with the agency, you can learn new skills, gain exposure to different work environments, and gain credibility and feedback from employers who can act as referees for future work. You might even be offered a standout permanent opportunity. Mark Smith, Group Managing Director of people2people, says, 'Awarding "Temp of the Month" is just one of the ways we show how much we appreciate our on-hire employees and the work that they do'.

One of the best elements of temporary employment is the ability to experience an environment before committing to it permanently. Many of our on-hire employees over the years have first worked with a business on a temporary basis and then been offered permanent employment. The unique advantage that this gives candidates is essentially a 'try before you buy' approach – they get to work in the environment first and see if they really like it. When you interview for a permanent job you don't always get that insight. Often it's two interviews and a phone call and you're ready to sign your career over for the next five to ten years! With temporary assignments, you can really assess culture, training, management, environment, values and ethics closely from the 'inside' before you commit.

Looking to progress your career or get your foot in the door? On-hire assignments can provide opportunities to enhance your career in ways that may not be possible with permanent work.

> **Case study**
>
> Alia was a logistics graduate who was seeking a permanent job as a Logistics Coordinator. She applied to many different companies, but the competition was fierce, and she kept getting knocked back in favour of candidates with more work experience. She registered with a recruitment agency and, although she had never considered temp work before, they found her a logistics coordinator assignment within a transport business. The company would normally go through a three-stage recruitment process for the permanent position, but after seeing how well Alia did her job and the positive attitude and work ethic that she brought, they decided to offer her a permanent job. Alia not only accepted the opportunity but went on to be promoted to a team leader position three years later.

The flexibility of on-hire employment allows you to choose which assignments you do and don't want to accept. In Australia there is also a casual loading of 25% to each hourly pay rate to cover annual and personal leave, which can often mean a little more pay in your bank account for the same job. If you're considering temporary or on-hire work, you should check out the relevant employment authority's website in your country, such as fairwork.gov.au, which provides advice on pay, conditions and entitlements. The Fair Work site even has a pay calculator so you can find out which modern award and pay rate applies to you.

On-hire permanent employment

Looking for the commitment of a full-time position, but seeking variety too? An on-hire permanent position can see you employed permanently by a recruitment agency which offers you on-hired work with a host workplace.

Case study

Elvin, a boilermaker, was offered permanent employment with a recruitment agency. He went out and worked at a mining company for a couple of years and then a manufacturing facility for another few years. Even though his work environment had changed, and so had the end host, his employment stayed continuous across both assignments. He had statutory leave entitlements such as personal leave, annual leave and long service leave. His employment relationship was with the agency and not the host; however, a shared responsibility existed for his work health and safety (WHS).

On-hire permanent work can be offered to you on a full-time or part-time basis. If you take up this form of employment, you are committing long-term to the recruitment agency. They will ensure that you are engaged in meaningful, ongoing work, and offered fair pay and conditions and quality work environments.

Contract work

Contract work is similar to temporary employment in that it is often related to a particular project, to cover leave, or to assist with an increase in workload. However, it is usually for a set period of time, such as six or twelve months, and has a specified end date. It provides a level of certainty around what length of time you will be working with the employer and allows you to plan for other employment when the contract ends.

Contract work can be offered directly by the employer or via a recruitment agency. The recruitment agency can either negotiate the contract for you and then offer you direct employment with the company you'll be working at, or offer you employment with the agency in an on-hire arrangement with the host. You can also be engaged as an independent contractor. Independent contractors can be classified as individuals or be associated with an incorporated company. Check with your recruitment agency regarding which type of contracting is being offered, as this can have an effect on who pays tax on your behalf, and other conditions.

Freelancing or gig work

Freelancing gives you the freedom to pick and choose work. Typically it can be a mixture of temporary, contract and casual work, as well as work that you might complete under your own business. The term 'gig work' is typically used for individuals undertaking a high proportion of work via on-demand websites, but can encompass a broad range of freelance and temporary work.

> **Case study**
>
> Jane is a copywriter. She has her own business, ABC Copywriting, through which she pitches work to companies and invoices them directly. She is also registered with a recruitment agency that offers her assignments from time to time. Lastly, she has a profile on a freelancing website where she bids for and completes work. All of these forms of freelance work make up her employment.

There are sites like Freelancer, Upwork, TaskRabbit and 99designs where employers post jobs and freelancers can bid on them. When engaging with these sites and others, it's a great idea to read the terms and conditions in full, understand whether an employment relationship exists and know what your entitlements are. In Australia, refer to fairwork.gov.au or your local employment authority to understand your rights. Some sites act simply as an introduction service between you and the employer, while other sites will actually become your employer and on-hire you to host companies.

Internships

Completing an internship can give you excellent work experience, exposure, networking and learning opportunities. In 2017, 78% of US-based university graduates completed an internship or apprenticeship, according to Accenture's *Gen Z Rising* report. Internships are great for university leavers, overseas candidates seeking local work experience and people changing careers. Internships in Australia can be paid or unpaid. If unpaid, ensure that you are completing the internship through an accredited program. Australia has a minimum wage for a reason – it helps to protect employees from exploitation and low pay. Unpaid internships are only available via student or vocational programs, or where no employment relationship exists. Visiting fairwork.gov.au is a great place to explore this further, or contact your local employment authority to understand the rules that apply in your country or region.

Apprenticeships

Want to earn a qualification while getting paid for your work? Apprenticeships are a great way to do this and to learn while you're on the job. Australianapprenticeships.gov.au provides a step-by-step guide to becoming an apprentice, and provides links to various training organisations where you can get started. You can shadow others in the profession, learn business-critical skills and gain experience with an employer straight away. An apprenticeship can be your 'foot in the door' to long-term ongoing employment in your chosen field.

Graduate programs

Your entry into a new organisation might be by way of a graduate program. Graduate programs can offer you exposure to new skills and concepts and the support that you need to develop successfully towards ongoing employment. Most graduate programs run for 12 to 24 months, with some organisations offering a guaranteed transition into a permanent role upon completion of the program. Often an organisation's objective in running a graduate program is to identify, train and develop future leaders. As a result, entry into some graduate programs can be competitive, with lengthy and detailed recruitment processes. Don't let this scare you, though. Preparation and focus, and following the advice in this book, can give you an edge during the graduate program recruitment process.

Self-employment

Starting and managing your own business can be very appealing when changing careers. It can be great when wanting to step out on your own, to facilitate freelance work or to create a path to employment. According to the Australian Small Business and Family Enterprise Ombudsman, there are more than 2.1 million small businesses in Australia, employing more than 4.7 million people and contributing $393 billion annually to the Australian economy.

To be self-employed in Australia you will need an Australian Business Number (ABN), which is an identifying number for the government and community, which you can obtain via the Australian Business Register. Of course, more importantly, you'll need a plan for your business and a strategy for growth, as well as a great deal of focus, energy and passion. Many successful businesses have started with a tiny idea, and maybe yours can too.

Fair pay and conditions

To ensure that you are paid correctly and treated fairly with appropriate conditions, you can research minimum wages and award conditions via government websites such as fairwork.gov.au in Australia. If you accept a job offer and later find that you are underpaid, gather information on what you should have been paid and raise the issue with your employer. If you are unable to come to a resolution, you can lodge a claim via the appropriate governing body or ombudsman in your country to help you seek fair pay and recourse for lost wages. Staying informed of your rights and responsibilities can help you gain employment with a quality employer with fair pay and conditions.

☕ Coffee break

We've explored Employer Value Propositions and benefits on offer to you. We've also looked at many forms of work, including permanent, temporary, on-hire, contract, apprenticeships, graduate programs and self-employment. For any employment relationship, you can expect a professional contract to be in place between you and your employer. Read all of the terms and conditions carefully and seek independent advice before you sign anything. Refer to chapter 14 to negotiate the right conditions for you. Whichever form of employment you choose, ensure it aligns with your career vision, goals and values. In preparation for submitting job applications, let's now look at setting up your online profile.

Part II
Your online profile

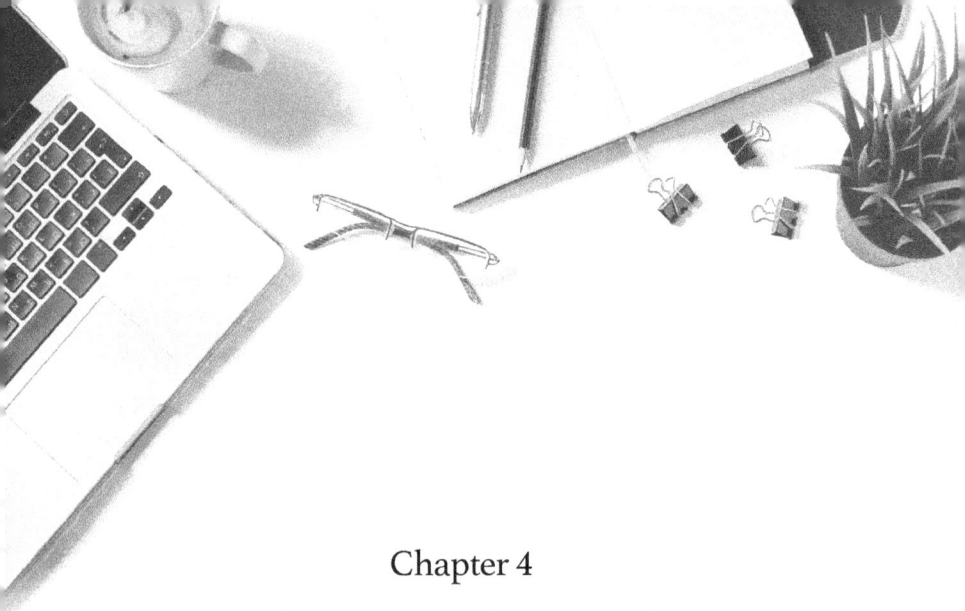

Chapter 4

Let's start with LinkedIn

- Create a professional LinkedIn profile.
- Show thought leadership and niche expertise.
- Attract prospective employers and engage your network.

Once upon a time you would send your CV off in the mail, but now employers want to research your background online at a time and place that suits them. Of course, you can do the same to research potential companies to work for. Employers are interested in your experience and how you present yourself, communicate online, discuss particular topics and engage with other people. Having a great online presence is key before pressing 'submit' on that job application.

Now that you've set your career goals, developed your Employee Value Proposition and know what you're looking for in an employer, it's time to start putting together your online profile.

You, online

Start by googling yourself. You may be surprised at what comes up. Is it the tweet you posted back in 2018 creatively expressing your thoughts about toast? Or is it a list of great blogs you've written? Professional social media pages? Excellent videos? News interviews?

Now is a great time to view your online presence from the perspective of a potential employer. You can make any personal accounts private, review profile pictures that can be seen publicly and decide which content you want a potential employer to see.

Reflection

I'll never forget back in 2007 when a client of mine called about a candidate, Rachel, who I had referred for a job. 'I can't hire her' he said, disappointed and frustrated.

I was confused. She was amazing – perfect for the job. Why wasn't he interested?

'Have you seen her Facebook page?' he asked.

'No', I said, thinking that looking at her Facebook would be quite intrusive.

'Well', he said, 'have a look now'.

Feeling very unsure and like I was invading Rachel's privacy, I reluctantly looked up her Facebook page. Fortunately, the person in the questionable pictures (which were publicly available) was not the person that I'd interviewed.

'That's not her', I said. Luckily the 'real' Rachel was not in those pictures and went on to get the job.

This was the moment that I realised that no information was 'off limits' to employers when candidates were applying for a job. I knew that anything publicly available would be found, assessed and considered as part of the candidate's job application, whether we as the agency liked it or not.

My advice about your online profile is pretty clear. *You* should be in control of the conversation about you. *You* should be able to pick and choose what an employer knows. And that conversation starts online. Your prospective employer will likely search for you online before they meet you. So, let's get started with LinkedIn, where you can showcase your professional profile and achievements.

Your LinkedIn profile

LinkedIn, launched in 2003, is the most commonly used professional networking site in the world, with over 740 million users. It's often the first place an employer looks when receiving your job application. To stand out, set up a profile that will complement your CV and market you well to a prospective employer.

First, create a profile, and fill out your contact details and initial information. Then add key details to the following sections to help you build your profile:

- Name
- Headline
- Current position
- Location
- Industry
- Contact information
- About
- Featured
- Activity
- Experience
- Education
- Licences and certificates
- Volunteer experience
- Skills and endorsements
- Recommendations
- Accomplishments
- Interests

The LinkedIn help section has great information that you can use to understand what to put in each section and how to use particular features.

Here are my top ten tips for creating a great LinkedIn profile that will make you stand out for the job that you *really* want.

1. Your headline should be clickable

Your headline articulates what you do, so if you're currently employed, it could contain your title, plus any post-nominals and the name of your employer. You could also add any awards or achievements such as 'Dean's List' or '100K+ Followers', or calls to action such as 'Tweet Me' or 'We're Hiring'. This has benefits beyond your job search too. What you 'do' isn't always conveyed well by your title, so you could choose to make it clearer. For example, if your title is *Administrator*, you could change your tagline on LinkedIn to 'Supporting a great sales team'.

In recent years it's become fashionable to have a headline with a fancy catchphrase, but be careful not to appear boastful or make it sound cheesy. If you're not sure and want to play it safe, stick with your actual current title, such as 'Executive Assistant at XYZ Company' or 'Student at ABC University'. If you're not currently employed and you really want to stand out to a recruiter, you could highlight your experience. For example:

> Sales Consultant 5+ years | Solar, Insurance, Health | Immediately Available

> Marketing Graduate (Honours) | Web Development | Copywriting | Graphic Design | Available Now

Note that some headlines can be cut short when you're posting activity, so make sure that you put the most important information first.

2. Use only photos that present you professionally

It can be tempting to use the most flattering photo that you have of yourself, but make sure that it is professional too. Having another person's body half cropped out of the picture, or a photo of you as a bridesmaid might be okay for Facebook, but you're better off choosing an alternative for LinkedIn.

You can either use a professional head shot or, if you don't have one ready to go, ask a friend to help you take one. Choose a plain background to keep the focus on you, nice lighting and a professional outfit that you would wear to work.

3. Your 'About' section is your Employee Value Proposition

Your EVP is what sells you well for a potential job, and the 'About' section on LinkedIn is where you can summarise it. You can highlight your values, thought leadership, experience, education, skills, achievements and vision. For example, your opening line might be something like this:

> 'With 15 years' experience in logistics and supply chain management, I'm passionate about developing strategies that reduce environmental impact, ensure sustainability and deliver profitability.'

And then you might go on to speak about previous education, skills and achievements.

> 'As a Graduate of the Australian Institute of Company Directors, I have board-level experience, and have recently managed the set-up of an international branch for XYZ company.'

You can also put a concise summary at the top of the *About* section with bullet points of your EVP key selling points. For example:

- 'MD, people2people Recruitment Victoria
- CEO, Infront Sports Consulting
- RCSA Professional Recruiter of the Year 2017
- Careers & Employment Media Commentator: ABC, Channel 7, Foxtel, 2UE, Nine Entertainment
- Speaker – World Employment Conference 2019, CPA Congress 2019
- RCSA Chairman – VIC/TAS Council
- #loveyourwork Ambassador and Business Mentor'

4. Use keywords and be searchable

When employers and recruiters are searching for appropriate candidates, they look for particular skills, systems, industries and experience. Adding keywords to your LinkedIn profile is a great way to ensure that you appear in the right searches and are available to be contacted by potential employers. You can list these in your 'About' summary section, headline, or under specific jobs that you've had.

Most people use a range of different systems and technology in their work, study and personal lives. It's not uncommon though for me to ask candidates the question, 'What systems and technology have you used?' and for the answer to be simply 'Microsoft Office'. Nine times out of ten the person has used at least a dozen other technology platforms. Here are some examples of technology, apps or software programs that you might have used and could possibly list on your LinkedIn page:

- **Accounting:** Xero, SAP, MYOB, Reckon, QuickBooks, NetSuite
- **Website development:** WordPress, Adobe Dreamweaver, Shopify, Weebly, Bluefish
- **Design:** Adobe programs, Architect 3D, Canva, Autodesk SketchBook
- **Presentation:** PowerPoint, Keynote, Prezi, Google Slides, Visme
- **Enterprise resource planning:** Oracle, NetSuite, Sage, SAP, Microsoft Dynamics, Salesforce
- **Social media and SEO:** AdWords, Facebook, Tiktok, Instagram, Snapchat, LinkedIn
- **Medical:** Zedmed, Medical Director, PrimaryClinic, Clinic to Cloud
- **Appointments:** Appointuit, Calendly, Timify, Acuity, Setmore
- **Video editing:** Apple iMovie, Lumen5, Pinnacle Studio, Adobe Premiere, Corel VideoStudio
- **Making music:** GarageBand, Cubase, Pro Tools, FL Studio, Ableton Live

There are many other applications and software programs that you might use, so think broadly and they can be a great addition to your LinkedIn profile.

5. Give recommendations

The best way to build your own profile is to help others build theirs. So instead of only *asking* for recommendations on LinkedIn, think about *giving* them first. You can expect nothing in return, but you might just find that you do get a few coming back your way. You can recommend colleagues, fellow students or alumni, suppliers and even clients. You can comment on how you know them, why you think they're great and why you enjoy interacting with them.

6. Get active

A LinkedIn profile is not a static page; it's a living, breathing representation of you. It can give insights into your interests, values and communication style. You can post your own content, such as a blog or article you have written, repost from a news, blog or social media site, or share someone else's content and credit them.

Posting content without interacting with other people, though, is like having a one-sided conversation. Instead, you can view and comment on other people's posts, like their content and share it too. If you're strategic about what you post, prospective employers can grow to understand your areas of expertise and how you might add value.

> **Reflection**
>
> An AFL Development Coach I was working with was keen to secure a more senior position as an Assistant Coach with another club. The problem was that his CV looked exactly the same as all of the other AFL coaches that were likely to apply for this type of role. He had applied in the past and missed out. After working with him to develop his Employee Value Proposition, we focussed on emphasising an area which would make him stand out. His strength was in coaching and developing ruckmen, but you would never know that if you

looked at his online presence. Over the next few months, this coach went about blogging on the subject of ruck technique, posting his views on social media about coaching ruckmen, and was even asked to speak on the topic at a conference. He updated his online profile and CV to reflect this specialisation and became known as an expert in the area. Sure enough, when the right club advertised an Assistant Coach vacancy and they were seeking a ruck specialist, he was the obvious choice. He not only got an assistant role but a Senior Assistant Coach position.

What are you an expert in, or what do you want to become known for? What sort of thought leadership do you have or want to develop? These are great questions to address when deciding which content you are going to post to help you get the job that you *really* want.

7. Personalise your LinkedIn URL

When you sign up to LinkedIn, you are randomly assigned a set of numbers and letters which make up part of the URL link that people click on to view your profile. You can update this to your name instead; for example, linkedin.com/in/erindevlin. It looks more professional, is searchable and is easy to read. Plus, if you are putting it on your CV (which you should) or publicising it elsewhere, it's certainly a lot easier to type in!

8. Use data, statistics and examples

If you say you increased sales or improved productivity, then give us a percentage and tell us by how much. If you say you've managed big projects, how big? To one person 'big' might mean a 5000-word university essay; to another it might mean the construction of a 17-storey office building. If you say your HR work has led to better retention, by what percentage did your employee turnover improve? Be specific. If you look at my LinkedIn profile, you'll see that I haven't just 'worked with athletes', I've worked with 'over 500 professional athletes on career transition and planning'. Being specific can help you clarify achievements and stand out to an employer.

9. Choose your words carefully

Social media amplifies your personality. Are you warm, friendly and approachable? Confident, competent and hard-working? Are you displaying the characteristics of someone who others will enjoy working with? Do you give an employer confidence that you can add value to their organisation?

When I'm reading a CV or online profile, I can easily spot the difference in attitude between two candidates who have exactly the same job. I do this simply by looking at the way that they describe their duties and responsibilities, and how they word their summary and achievements. For example, two retail sales assistants might describe some of their duties as follows:

Candidate A:	Candidate B:
• dealing with customers	• helping customers and providing excellent service
• hanging up clothes	• proactively managing stock and merchandising
• handling difficult people	
• pushing sales	• answering queries and providing solutions
	• meeting and exceeding sales targets and KPIs

Who do you think will get the job?

In your summary, posts, recommendations and interactions on LinkedIn, do you come across as positive, proactive and hard-working? This is what employers will be looking for. They will be able to get a very strong feel for your personality via your LinkedIn profile and activity, and by looking at your other social media sites.

Additionally, when engaging with a prospective employer on LinkedIn, it's a good idea to include a message with your contact request invitation. You might say that you are interested in the business that they work for and that you'd like to add them as a professional contact on LinkedIn. Communication on LinkedIn is usually formal but friendly and a great place to show your positive attitude.

10. Be your future self

The best candidates I have worked with have a clear idea of the job that they want to secure in the future. Even if this changes over time, they have a goal, a vision and a road map to get there. On your LinkedIn profile, try to view everything you write through the lens of your future self. Let's say you want to be in a management position in the next five years. What would you, as the manager, say when you write that post? How would you word it? What would the tone be? That's the tone you want to have.

This is the advice that I give to candidates regarding how they interact with their colleagues, how they present themselves and what battles they pick. Would your future-manager self choose that course of action? Would they advise their colleagues in that way? What will happen when a promotion opportunity comes up? Will your colleagues think you are the obvious choice for the job or not a chance? Position yourself well now for that future promotion or job opportunity.

> ### ☕ Coffee break
>
> We've taken a look at your online profile and explored ways to help you stand out. Whether it's getting the right headline, photo or profile summary, there are many ways to do this. Ensure that your EVP is clearly communicated and that you are engaging well with your network. Show your personality and positive attitude, and use data, statistics and examples to back up your achievements. You've now set up your LinkedIn profile, presented yourself professionally and started to find ways to stand out. But before you begin applying for jobs, it's time to get your other social media profiles in shape and build your personal brand online.

Chapter 5

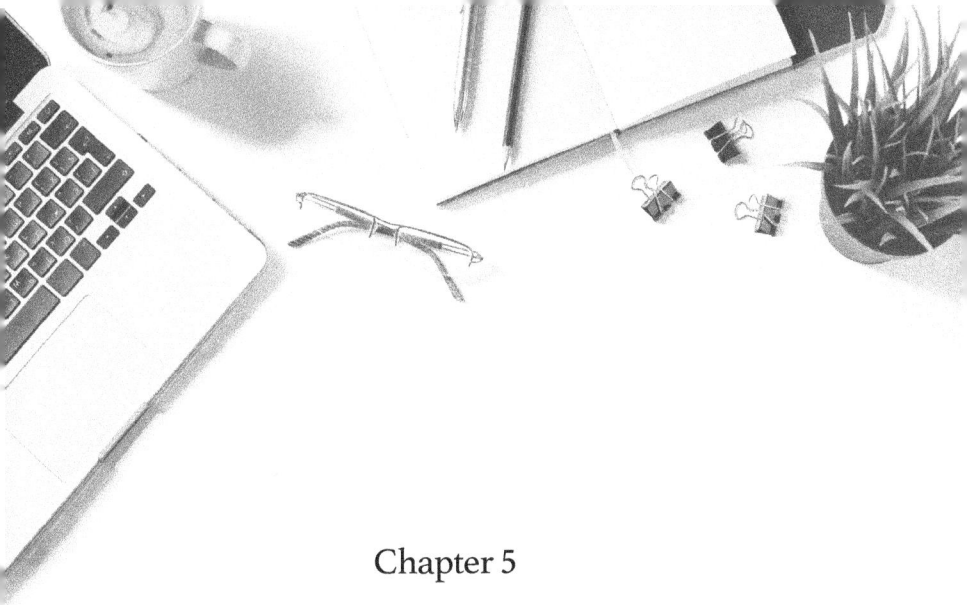

Build your personal brand online

- Set personal branding goals and create engaging profiles.
- Develop a career-focussed content marketing strategy.
- Attract potential employers and recruiters online.

'I have to be seen to be believed.'

~ Queen Elizabeth II

When looking to secure a promotion or a new job, building a strong personal brand online is key. Seventy per cent of employers use social media to screen candidates during the recruitment process, according to a 2017 CareerBuilder survey. Personal branding can position you as a subject-matter expert, thought leader and valuable individual. Prospective employers aren't looking for average performance; every time they hire, their goal is to raise or match the quality of employees in their organisation. Having a strong brand online can showcase your knowledge, expertise and ideas. It can also reveal your level of influence and the extent of your contact networks. A comprehensive network of contacts can be valuable to an employer who is looking to promote their business services and products. It gives them more reach and by hiring you, a ready-made audience.

Whether you're a fresh graduate or an experienced professional, there is plenty of content that you can create, share and engage with that will enhance your personal brand. You'll want to be present across multiple platforms and forums. Let's look at why you should build your brand, who your audience could be and how to set up a great online presence. We'll also explore where to post, how often, and what content is best.

Personal branding goals and target audience

First, be clear about your reason for building a brand online and link this to your career goals. It might be that you'd like to work towards a particular position or promotion, or maybe you are currently applying for jobs. Next, decide on your target audience. Is it a prospective employer or your current CEO? Who is it that you want reading your posts and taking notice? Be clear on your audience now, and this will help you tailor relevant content and make you stand out.

Case study

Jacinta is an Account Manager with an advertising agency. In the future she would like to become a Group Account Director. In order to build her brand and credibility online, she starts to post articles about marketing principles, creative strategy and leadership. She builds up a following of marketing professionals, including leaders of advertising agencies who are potential employers. Jacinta is approached by two recruiters and an advertising agency who are looking to hire – they have noticed her. Her own manager also notes her engagement online, her level of influence and positive interactions. Recognising the potential that Jacinta has, her manager quickly recommends her for an internal leadership program. She is put on a path to management opportunities. Jacinta's employment prospects and opportunity for promotion are now both very strong.

Refer back to your career goals and values from Chapters 1 and 2 to inform your personal branding objectives and target audience. Let's say for example that you're passionate about environmental sustainability, and you also want to use your design skills and education. You might like to define your ultimate audience as a prospective employer who hires designers that create environmentally sustainable office fit-outs. To build your credibility as a top candidate in this area, you'll want to curate and post content about design *and* environmental sustainability. Look at your own career goals and decide how personal branding can help you advance them. There will be people who can support your career direction too, so connect with them online and start to develop your professional network. You can list your personal branding goals and target audience here:

PERSONAL BRANDING GOALS

_____
_____
_____
_____
_____
_____
_____

TARGET AUDIENCE

_____
_____
_____
_____
_____
_____
_____

Where should I post?

The top four platforms for employment and business engagement are LinkedIn, Instagram, Twitter and YouTube. Facebook and Snapchat are also big business, but I would recommend setting these to private and keeping them for personal use only; employers will only be able to view what you have made public or available to them. I recommend setting up your LinkedIn profile using Chapter 4 as a guide, and consider creating a professional Twitter account. Instagram is another site that employers will look at if you've made it public. If you do have a public account, make sure that it is dedicated to professional content and keep your personal profile private. Alternatively, you can use the 'close contacts' function on Instagram to share personal content only with specific followers.

If you have a YouTube channel, consider how prospective employers might view it. If you're applying for IT helpdesk jobs and your YouTube channel is where you troubleshoot computer problems, then that will work to your advantage. If you have a cooking channel and are applying for executive assistant positions, that's fine too, as long as the content on the cooking channel will reflect positively on you and on a prospective employer. After all, once employed, you will be an extension of their brand and image.

You can enhance your personal branding online through posting on additional sites, but bear in mind that employers will typically only view two or three platforms as part of their research during a recruitment process. You might be saying something spectacular on Spreely, but the chances of a prospective employer seeing it are slim. There are particular sites that are a must-have when personal branding for certain professions, such as TikTok for singers, Architizer for architects or TankChat for people in oil and logistics.

Be selective about which sites are relevant to your personal branding goals and whether the platform delivers benefits in line with them.

Here is a broader list of social media sites, to give you some ideas:

LinkedIn	Reddit	Spreely
Instagram	ReverbNation	Discord
Twitter	Care2	WT.Social
Facebook	Nextdoor	Triller
YouTube	Upstream	Elpha
Snapchat	Classmates	Yubo
Tumblr	Buzznet	PopBase
Pinterest	Meetup	StartupNation
Flickr	Quora	

Many people ask why I choose to have a professional Instagram (@erin_devlin_). I see Instagram as meeting in the middle of professional and personal. It allows prospective employers, clients and contacts to see you as a person, not just as an employee, and brings a fun, fresh, visual perspective to your content. As an example, I use Instagram to share team successes, birthdays, videos and 'behind-the-scenes' stories, along with job opportunities that we are currently recruiting for. People connect with me as a person and learn about my life, while getting to know my professional interests too. They find out what it's like to work with me and can understand my interests, goals, values and the environment that I like to work in. Instagram is a great forum for you to professionally showcase visual elements of your work, interests, values and personality to a prospective employer. Maintaining personal and professional accounts separately is always a great way do this.

Twitter, in contrast, is like a busy social function where everyone is having different conversations. You can tune in and out depending on what interests you. With tweets not allowed to be more than 280 characters, comments are brief and the pace is high. It's a great forum for you to follow and engage with prospective employers and contacts, voice your professional opinions, encourage others and share content and ideas. As with all social media platforms where your profile is publicly available, keep it professional and in line with your career goals and values.

Setting up a great profile

The ideal time to prepare your social media profile on each platform is *before* you start to add contacts. You don't want to show up to the party before you're even ready. Take some time to select the right handle, photo, cover picture and bio, and share some posts before you make any connections. People are more likely to accept contact requests if they can get a feel for the content that they can expect in the future.

First, understand the culture of each platform. For example, LinkedIn is used mostly for professional content, job searching and company updates. Instagram is about posting quality photos, quotes, videos and stories. Twitter is like a big conversation and features news, blogs, and quick, informative, opinionated or witty comments. Knowing the mood of each platform can help you create a great profile, as can the following suggestions:

1. Upload a friendly but professional photo and cover image.
2. Select a handle that is easily searchable like @your_name.
3. Write a great bio that is optimised for search engines.

Use keywords that employers would search for if they were looking to hire you. For example, if you're an occupational therapist, you might include 'occupational therapist' as a keyword, but also 'OT' or 'occupational therapy'. It gives you a better chance of being found depending on what keywords are searched for.

When employers and recruiters are looking to fill a position, they often use tools like Followerwonk to search Twitter, Instagram and Facebook profiles. Adding keywords to your professional social media accounts can be the difference between being called about your ideal job and not being called at all.

In your bio, be engaging, concise and energising, and make the reader want to follow you. For example, you might say 'Follow me for OT advice, insights and wellbeing tips'. You can cross-promote your LinkedIn profile by providing the link below your bio. Add your location to ensure employers pick your profile up in location-specific searches. Lastly, make it human – people connect with people, and look for fun, interesting content that can inform them or brighten their day.

Who should I connect with?

Start by building your network with people you know who might be interested in your content. Connect with friends, family, people from school, university and previous workplaces. You never know who they might be connected to or where they work now. They may even be able to influence your career, or maybe you can help them. Look to build your target audience by following companies and people who resonate with your career goals, values and interests. They might just follow you back.

You can join professional groups on LinkedIn, Facebook and Twitter. You can search by keywords relevant to your profession or look for industry groups and associations. If you join groups on Facebook, make sure that your privacy settings are altered so that they cannot see your profile. If you find someone on Facebook that you'd like to connect with for professional purposes, search for them on LinkedIn or Twitter and connect with them on there instead.

Once you have established your initial social media audience, you will want to attract contacts who can positively influence your career. Remember it's a two-way street, though. Make sure you can add value to them by posting articles of interest, supporting their ideas and engaging with their content. If you are going to apply for jobs where a network of contacts is advantageous, such as in sales, marketing or media, then growing a larger audience is helpful. There's no point being connected to just anybody though – ensure that you connect with people who will find your posts as interesting as you find theirs. The best way to grow your connections and followers is to post the right content.

Let's look at content marketing strategies now.

What type of content should I post?

The most important aspect of building a brand online is authenticity. Research reported in a 2008 *Journal of Counseling Psychology* article showed that authentic people had better relationships and more personal growth. They also reported greater happiness, positive emotions and higher self-esteem – all very important attributes for someone seeking the right job. Remain true to yourself and create and post content that genuinely represents who you are. You will be attractive to the right employers with aligned values. If they resonate with your content, chances are that they will share some common views, and that's a great foundation for an employment relationship.

On social media, people follow people, not stiff or overly engineered brands. They enjoy engaging with content that is fresh, real and invigorating. Posts that spark ideas, get people thinking and elicit a smile are a great foundation for your content strategy. Here are the top ten organic post types that you can use to enhance your personal brand:

1. **Blog posts:** Write an article on a topic that you're interested in and that aligns with your area of expertise. LinkedIn has a blog feature that you can use for this purpose, and it brings potential employers back to your professional profile. Simply click on 'Home' and below 'Start a post' select 'Write article'.

2. **Photos:** Share photos of professional events, your work environment, designs, work you've completed or people you're meeting with. You might even be out and about in the city and share where you're going, or what a great day it is. Provide a caption which speaks to your area of expertise and values, and use hashtags to support your message.

3. **Videos:** Create a tutorial, informative or behind-the-scenes video that helps or entertains your followers. There are free teleprompters like CuePrompter which help you to deliver the right message and engage directly with your audience.

4. **News:** Share a news article directly from a credible news site such as ABC, Forbes, the BBC or *The Economist*, or aggregators like HuffPost.

5. **Stories:** Give followers a window into your life by using the 'story' function on Instagram and LinkedIn. Stories are ephemeral and disappear after 24 hours, so 'in the moment' content is perfect. Focus on content that projects you as a subject-matter expert and aligns with your career goals.

6. **Polls:** Engage your followers with a poll that poses a question relevant to your area of expertise. A banker might post, 'Will the RBA raise interest rates today?' while a childcare worker might post, 'What's your favourite activity for toddlers?' For each poll, provide multiple options to select.

7. **Questions:** Similar to polls, you can engage your audience with a question that encourages their participation. It's a great way for you to get followers thinking and for you to interact with their comments.

8. **Quotes:** This might be your own statement or where you are crediting someone else. You can make the post more appealing by overlaying the quote on a visual tile. Steer clear of cheesy content and stick with inspirational, uplifting and lighthearted quotes.

9. **Memes:** Some of the best memes out there on social media are engaging, funny, and thought-provoking. A quick wit and good humour are well placed in business and, depending on the type of humour, can often be a sign of intelligence and employability. Respect and taste are key to getting this right.

10. **Livestreams:** If you're brave enough to speak to your followers live and have a well-planned script, you can use livestreams. They trigger different notifications and can help you reach new audiences. Livestreams can be very engaging, and allow connections to ask you questions and make comments in real time.

In addition to your own content, a large part of what you post should be shared from others. People love to have their content liked and, best of all, shared. It's the biggest compliment you can give them online. It's also a great way to engage with prospective employers, encourage others and promote positive ideas. It develops your relationship with the person posting, builds your credibility and helps others. Remember to credit the original poster. On LinkedIn, simply use the 'share' button at the bottom of each post. On Twitter, use the 'retweet' function, and on Instagram you'll need a purpose-built app like 'Repost' to share content with the original poster's handle included.

There are many ways that you can build your connections and engage with the right audiences on social media. You can like, comment and share content from others. You can join in on question-and-answer sessions, answer polls, send replies to stories, recommend people, endorse contacts for skills and follow companies. Using hashtags allows users to search for content and easily find you. You can also cross-promote your social media accounts by sharing your Twitter handle on LinkedIn and your Instagram handle on YouTube.

When should I post?

Think about the timing of your posts to ensure optimal reach to your audience. When are they likely to be scrolling through social media? At work? At home? On the train? It's best to try to reach your audience when they are online and listening. In 2020 Sprout Social looked at data from more than 25,000 customers' Instagram activity and found that Wednesday at 11 a.m. and Friday at 10 a.m. are the best times to post for optimal reach and engagement. They found that Wednesday is the best day overall and that the most consistent engagement happens from Tuesday through to Thursday from 10 a.m. to 3 p.m.

Consider the type of content that you post at particular times. Most people don't want a heavy work-related post the minute that they finish their workday, so choosing relaxed, thoughtful content could help match their mood. Energising, inspirational content is great first thing in the morning, with ideas, polls and questions throughout the day.

You can use social media posting and scheduling tools to make your life easier. Hootsuite, Buffer and TweetDeck are great examples and often have free versions available for small amounts of usage. They allow you to post to multiple social media platforms at particular times. You can schedule posts in advance and ensure that they go out when you want them to.

How often should I post?

Frequent and engaging content can raise your profile. Keeping the balance is important though, as time is a factor and it's best not to overdo it. People will tune out if they feel spammed or start to skip your content if it's too frequent. So, what is the frequency of content that you can post to create a healthy brand online and stand out to employers? As a guide, I would share content as follows on average:

- Organic post: twice per week
- Own blog or video: once per month
- Sharing other people's content: once per week
- Engaging with other people's comments: daily

If you work in marketing or digital media, increase the frequency of your posts and interactions, as being highly engaged online is central to your employability. If you're a journalist, then Twitter is a key platform for regular engagement, and if you're a photographer or creative professional then frequent Instagram posts or stories will benefit you. Frequency of engagement and posts will also depend on whether you have access to content created by your current organisation or whether you are creating it from scratch. Being visible with quality content and interaction, and at the right times, makes you more attractive to a prospective employer.

> ### ☕ Coffee break
>
> Now that you've set up your online profile and are posting and interacting regularly, you have a much greater chance of being found by the right employer. You are also more appealing as a prospective employee because of your network and position as a subject-matter expert. If you have tailored your content well, focussed on your career goals and amplified your values, then you will have improved your job prospects. As a thought leader or expert in your field, no matter how fresh to the workforce or experienced you are, you will definitely stand out to a potential employer. When they are looking at applications and search for you online, they will notice that you are a true professional, an expert and most likely a pleasure to work with. That's appealing for any employer. Before you start applying for jobs, though, there are a few more steps that we need to take. First, let's prepare your curriculum vitae (CV) or resume.

Part III

CVs, resumes and cover letters

Chapter 6

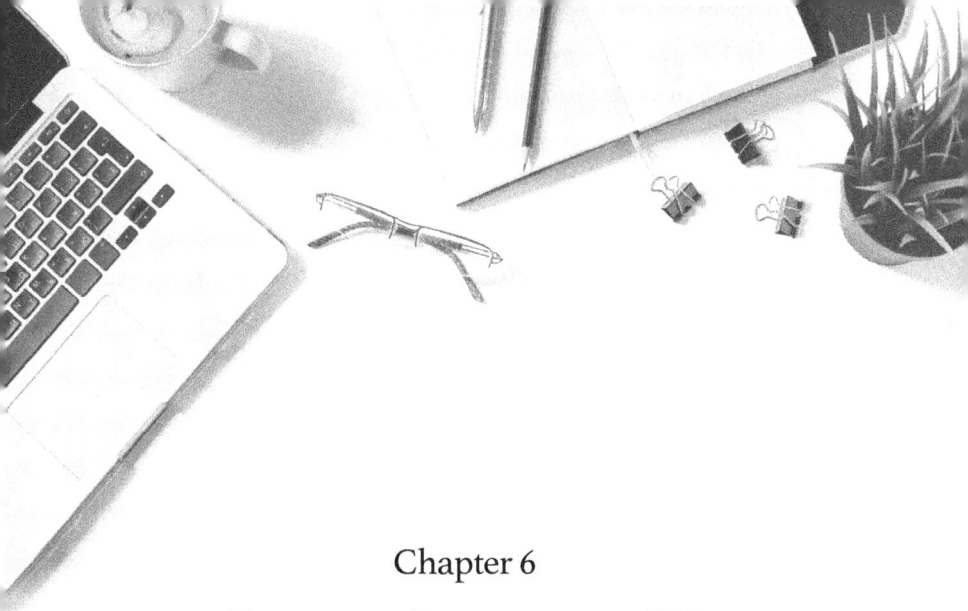

Put together a great CV

- Impress with your CV in eight seconds.
- Communicate your Employee Value Proposition.
- Show an employer why they should interview you.

A great curriculum vitae (CV) or resume is what can get your foot in the door for an interview. And when a study by the UK's National Citizen Service tells us that 8.8 seconds is the average time an employer spends looking at your CV before moving on, it pays to get it right! Even though predictions have been made that CVs will no longer be needed in the future, they are not outdated yet. Hiring managers and recruiters like to have a full and detailed understanding of your work experience, education and skills. It's why it's usually the first thing that you're asked to send when applying for a job.

Let's look at the most important elements of putting together a great CV and how to ensure that you're noticed. Throughout the remainder of the book, for ease we will use the words 'CV' and 'resume' interchangeably, but there is actually a difference.

CV or resume?

A CV is a detailed record of your education, qualifications, work experience and skills, while a resume is short (one- or two-page) overview of the same information. (*Résumé* is a French word meaning 'summary'.) A CV is most commonly used for job applications in Australia, the UK, Ireland and New Zealand, while a resume is almost always used in the US and Canada. Americans and Canadians would typically use a CV when applying for academic, medical or scientific positions to list details of credentials, certifications, research experience and professional memberships. In Asia, Europe, the Middle East or Africa, employers usually expect a CV, often with a photo. Many organisations in Australia will accept a resume format too, but CVs are much more common and often preferred.

The foundation of your CV and resume is your Employee Value Proposition, which we discussed in detail in Chapter 2. You can emphasise the aspects of your experience, skills and education that will be most relevant to an employer. Additionally, here are the four most important principles of putting together a great CV:

1. Articulate your EVP and key information on the front page.
2. Design for easy reading and use keywords.
3. Articulate achievements and what you can offer clearly.
4. Inspire the reader to call you for an interview.

What is the purpose of your CV?

To get an interview! It's simple. Give clear, concise information that makes the reader want to pick up the phone and invite you in. Throughout my career I have reviewed hundreds of thousands of CVs. The candidates that make it easy for recruiters and employers are the candidates who tell their reader who they are *on the front page*. If an employer has to dig backwards to find out you actually have an honours degree in psychology, you may miss out on the job.

So, if there is one thing that you should remember from this chapter, it's this: Tell us who you are and what you can offer *on the first page*.

What should you put on the first page of your CV?

1. Title or tagline

Target positions directly by listing a title or tagline underneath your name. Tailor it to the position you are applying for; keep it truthful and succinct. Here are some examples of how using a title might look:

Your Name
Graphic Designer

Your Name
Fibre Optics Technician

Your Name
Registered Nurse

Your Name
Policy Analyst

You can expand this to a tagline; for example, you might say 'Payroll Manager with SAP, Microsoft Dynamics and Chris21'. A tagline is a catchphrase used typically in advertising. You can use it to highlight who you are and what you bring to the table. Avoid flashy or boastful statements such as 'Sales professional who exceeds targets by 20% every time'. Making big claims upfront can be a lot to live up to and may be a turn-off for employers. Instead, highlight key experience, systems, industry knowledge and skills that employers might be looking for. Here are some great tagline examples which are tailored to the job:

Receptionist with 3+ years' experience in professional services
Medical assistant with Zedmed and MedicalDirector experience
Marine biologist specialising in jellyfish species

You can also use a spaced format such as:

Front Desk Manager | Five Star Hotels | 8+ Years' Industry Experience

Tax Accountant | MYOB, Xero | 4+ Years' Experience

Commercial Property Agent | 120+ properties sold | 10+ years Canberra Market

2. Personal details

List your contact details right up the top of your CV, including your mobile number, email address and the suburb, state and postcode that you live in. This helps recruiters contact you quickly and understand how far you might be from the job location. You can also add links to your professional social media profiles, including LinkedIn. If you work in a creative industry, provide a link to your online portfolio, personal website or showreel. Here's an example of how you might list your contact details.

Alisha Patel

- 📞 0400 000 000
- ✉ yourname@yourprovider.com.au
- 🏠 Your Suburb, State, 0000
- 💼 linkedin.com/in/yourname
- 📷 @your_instagram_handle
- 💼 www.yourportfoliolink.com

Under your contact details, you can include key personal information if it's relevant to the job, such as visa details or whether you have a full driver's licence. Don't list your age or marital status – this is old-fashioned, not relevant to the job and can also expose you to the risk of discrimination, which we will discuss further in Chapter 7.

Of the thousands of CVs that we receive at people2people weekly, probably less than 1% include a photo. It is uncommon in Australia, but more common in the Middle East, Asia, Europe and Africa. Including a photo is a personal choice. If you work in a field such as acting or dancing then it may be a prerequisite, but if you are an accountant or farmhand, your appearance is irrelevant to the job. If you would like to avoid the risk of discrimination based on your appearance, leave your photo off. You can keep the employer focussed on your experience, skills and abilities. If they look up your social media profiles, of course they are likely to see your photo there, but by that stage they will already have an idea of your Employee Value Proposition.

3. Write a great profile summary or career objective

Sometimes known as a 'personal statement', your profile summary or career objective should be clear, concise and tailored to the job, and should get straight to the point. It gives a prospective employer an insight into your experience, skills, personality and career focus. Here is my three-step formula:

1. **Who you are:** Include your profession, years of experience and what you specialise in.
2. **What you can offer:** Elaborate further on key positions you've held, and industries and systems experience.
3. **Your career focus:** Clarify what you're looking to achieve with your next career move.

Ensure that all points relate to the job that you are applying for and highlight your most relevant experience, skills and interests. Here are two profile examples using the formula above and the jobs they are applying for:

Payroll Manager

A payroll manager with six years' experience, I specialise in high-volume payroll processing, award interpretation and multiple pay runs. I have supported organisations in FMCG, healthcare and retail, and bring knowledge of Chris21, SAP and KeyPay. I would like to join a progressive, innovative organisation, managing the payroll function end to end, where I can add value and grow within the organisation.

Environmental Health Officer (Local Government)
I am an environmental scientist, passionate about improving recycling processes and facilities within Australian cities. Having completed a Bachelor of Environmental Science majoring in chemistry, I established my career working at ABC recycling facility, where I have developed strong knowledge of recycling systems over the past five years. I am looking to contribute my skills and experience to a local government team.

4. Summarise your career

Give a concise summary of the positions you have held throughout your career in list format on the front page. Here is an example:

Director	LMN Board	2016 – Current
Engineering Manager	ABC Company	2015 – Current
Manager Eng. Solutions	ABC Company	2013 – 2015
Design Engineer	XYZ Company	2008 – 2013
Design Engineer	QRS Company	2006 – 2008
Engineering Graduate	TUV Company	2004 – 2006

This gives the reader a quick snapshot of your experience and career trajectory.

5. Include qualifications

If you have a qualification or certificate that is relevant to the job, such as a university degree or trade certificate, include it on the front page. If your education is limited, move this section to the back of your CV. Only include recent, relevant education on the front page, and detail other professional development later in your CV. Include the qualification name, the institution that you completed it at and the year when you finished. For example:

Bachelor of Science
The University of Adelaide, 2018

If you are listing more than one qualification, list them chronologically backwards; that is, put your most recent education at the top and older education below. Courses that you completed in 2015, for example, should be lower on the list than education completed in 2020.

6. Highlight awards and achievements

If you have won an award, secured a sporting or industry record or have other key highlights you would like the reader to know upfront, then include an 'Awards' or 'Highlights' section on the front page of your CV with a list below such as:

Tony Staley Award 2020
Community Broadcasting Association (CBAA)

Television Program of the Year 2017
National Community Television Awards

Or you can feature a bullet-point-list highlight reel instead of a fuller profile summary. It should list key experience, skills, education and achievements relevant to the job and be an articulation of your EVP or key selling points. Include:

- years of experience
- awards that you've won
- industries that you've worked in
- specialist skills or languages
- systems that you've used
- licences, visas or availability.

For example:

15 years' construction management experience
Awarded 'Best Safety Leadership Program' at the National Safety Awards, 2021

Commercial, residential and large-scale project experience
Engineering background and qualifications
Fluent in Mandarin and basic Cantonese
Proficient with SAGE 100, Architect 3D, STACK and CAD
First-aid qualified, heavy machinery and forklift licences current

When an employer receives over 300 applications for a job and many of them have the required experience, how do they decide who to interview? Specialist skills can make all the difference, including computer systems that you are trained in or languages that you can speak. If an employer doesn't have to train you on the computer system that they use, that will be a huge plus. If international liaison with stakeholders is required, then speaking another language could certainly make you stand out; research the company that you are applying for and see if they have global operations, offices, clients or suppliers.

7. List key skills

When your CV is parsed into applicant tracking systems, it is usually scanned for keywords and will rank you as a candidate based on these. Recruiters will also search CV databases with key phrases like 'Switchboard AND Reception'. Include a section that lists skills relevant to the job and addresses criteria directly from the job advertisement or position description. For example:

Employer seeking a receptionist:	Your skills list might include:
'We are seeking a candidate with strong Microsoft PowerPoint experience, data entry skills and excellent customer service.'	<ul><li>Advanced Microsoft Word</li><li>Advanced Microsoft PowerPoint</li><li>Alphanumeric data entry</li><li>Customer service</li><li>Communication</li><li>Reception management</li><li>Switchboard coordination</li></ul>

8. Note relevant certificates or memberships

If particular certificates, memberships or checks are required for the job, note those that you hold already on the front page of your CV. For example, for many jobs in Australia, you will require a national police clearance certificate or a Working with Children Check (WWCC). Obtain these in advance if you can and list them upfront.

Show your commitment to high-quality standards and professional development by listing memberships to industry associations, chambers of commerce or business groups. If you're looking for inspiration for associations and business groups to get involved with, visit australianchamber.com.au where the Australian Chamber of Commerce and Industry lists over 160 Australian business groups. (Some overseas equivalents are listed in the 'Useful websites' section at the back of this book.)

Beyond the first page you can start to elaborate on your work experience and achievements. Let's explore this now.

Work experience and achievements

Work experience is the largest and most significant part of your CV, and should include positions that you've held, companies that you've worked for, dates of employment, duties and achievements. You can also call this section 'Professional Experience'. As with education, list your most recent engagements chronologically backward. Start with your most recent position, list it at the top under your heading and provide details of older positions below. For each position list the title you held, the company you worked for and when you worked there. Share your title first before the company, because a prospective employer will be more interested in this information initially. Be sure to include months in your dates of employment – working from 2019 to 2021, which appears to be 'two years', is very different to working from December 2019 to January 2021, which is just over one year. If you are still working at the organisation listed, then list the start date and 'current' instead of the end date.

If a former employer has changed its name due to a merger, acquisition or rebrand, list both the current name of the business – so that a prospective employer can look them up – as well as the former name of the organisation. Summarise positions where appropriate. For example, if you had four part-time jobs during university, you could summarise these with a heading such as 'Part-time employment during study'. Underneath provide the title, company and dates of employment for each job.

Company description

Include a short description of the company which gives the reader an understanding of its size and location, the scope of the organisation and what it does. To illustrate this, you could include the number of employees, office locations, specialisations, brands, products or services, and even awards. You can also provide a link to the company's website. Here's an example of what this might look like:

> *General Manager, People and Culture*   *February 2012 to present*
> ABC Organisation
> www.abcorganisation.com
>
> ABC Organisation is a multinational chemicals manufacturer operating in 12 countries and headquartered out of Boston, Massachusetts, USA. Listed in the Top 100 Fastest-Growing Companies by Fortune.com, ABC Organisation supplies to some of the world's largest health, laboratory, food, agriculture and manufacturing organisations worldwide.

Responsibilities

Showcase the depth of your experience and capabilities by listing key duties and responsibilities next. As you get further back in your experience, you can reduce the amount of information included for each position. Condense your responsibilities into the top seven or eight and use bullet points for clarity. Combine similar duties into the one sentence, such as 'Planning and delivering training sessions for new and existing team members'. Use keywords to make it easier for employers to find critical skills.

Avoid two- or three-word sentences such as 'Customer service' or 'Accounts reconciliation'. Instead use a proactive tone; for example, 'Providing a high level of customer service' or 'Accurately reconciling accounts and updating records'. It paints a clearer picture of your true responsibilities and, by using descriptive words like 'high level' and 'accurately', highlights your focus on quality and doing your job well.

Use a consistent verb tense and avoid switching between the two. It's not uncommon for employers to see duties listed in the past tense like 'Led and developed…' and then in the next sentence the present tense 'Create and deliver'. It's subtle, but it can be distracting for the reader and speaks to your attention to detail. Show that you are careful and thorough in your work by being consistent. Use the present tense for a position that you currently hold and the past tense for older positions. Here's a sample duties list for a Senior Assistant AFL Coach:

Key responsibilities:
- Leading and developing a team of coaches and acting as an adviser to the Senior Coach
- Ensuring that the football club program runs smoothly
- Taking a key role in developing and supporting the leadership group
- Providing coaching and technical strategy relating to all areas of the game
- Undertaking opposition analysis and presenting information to players
- Reviewing game trends and incorporating strategy into the game
- Coaching ruck technique for the team with a focus on high performance
- Developing pre-season and in-season training programs
- Undertaking performance reviews with team members

- Developing strong relationships with departments
- Participating in list management meetings and providing advice on player selection.

Achievements

Articulating achievements well is the most important aspect of your CV. Employers will want to know what you have worked on in the past and whether you've been successful. Achievements can highlight this information and show what you are capable of in the future. In Chapter 2, we discussed achievements in detail and how to formulate them as part of your EVP. Now is a great time to revisit this section and refresh your thinking. Recruiters and employers want to understand how you've added value to past employers – it gives them confidence that you can add value to their organisation too. You've probably achieved a lot more than you give yourself credit for. So, let's look at your achievements and how we list them for maximum impact.

Under each position, below your Key Responsibilities list, provide two or three key achievements per position, or more for recent roles. Qualify and quantify these by using facts, data and outcome-driven language. You can also use the S.T.A.R. method, which stands for:

- Situation
- Task
- Action
- Result

In other words:

- What was the situation?
- What was the task?
- What action did you take to achieve it?
- And what was the result?

If you've written your duties well, this will have already set up the 'situation' and 'task' context for your achievements. This leaves you to articulate in your achievements the action you took and what the result was. For example, in your duties section you might have responsibilities as an engineer such as:

> 'Designing structurally sound foundations for residential homes
>
> Managing the materials budget effectively'

Then in your 'Achievements' section you might say:

> 'Identified a new design which enhanced the strength of foundations by 5% and delivered a materials budget saving of 16%'

By providing the context, the objectives, the action you took and the results achieved, you are showing a prospective employer how outcome-focussed you are. When competition is fierce, listing duties alone is not enough to get you through the door for an interview. Take the time to articulate your achievements and show the value that you can deliver.

Referees

List details of referees at the end of your CV. If you prefer to give contact details of referees at a later stage, then provide names and positions only or write 'Available on request'. Make sure that referees are people who you've been accountable to in the past. This might include previous managers or, if your work experience is limited, then your university course coordinator, lecturers, previous teachers or coaches are suitable.

For each referee provide their name, title, position, mobile number *and* email address. An email address allows recruiters and employers to schedule a time to speak, which can help avoid reference-checking delays. If the referee has changed jobs since you worked with them, list their current position *and* the former position where you were accountable to them. You can also provide context for how you know them; for example, 'Direct Manager for volunteer work at XYZ'. Here's a full referee example:

Brenda Algave
CEO of ABC Corporation
Former Managing Director of XYZ Organisation
M: 0400 000 000   E: hername@provider.com

Optional sections on your CV

Professional development

In the earlier 'Education' or 'Qualifications' section, include only formal certified education where you have had to pass a significant test or exam/s to achieve completion. Professional development is broader and encompasses any formal training that you have undertaken that has contributed to furthering your skills and experience. You can include webinars, seminars, masterclasses, short courses, conferences, mentoring and internal company training.

List the name of the qualification or professional development engagement, along with the institution that delivered it and the date of completion. There is no need to include the years that you attended the institution, just the date that you finished and received your certificate. For example:

Leadership Program
ABC Science Company, 2020

'A Culture Masterclass' Webinar
American Association for the Advancement of Science, 2020

Clinical Trials Fundamentals
Monash University, 2019

Biodiversity and Conservation Conference
ConferenceSeries LLC Ltd, 2019

Conference presentations

If you are an academic, researcher or subject-matter expert, you may have presented at local or international conferences. Include details of the topic of your presentation, the conference at which you presented it and the year when this occurred. Showing that you've been a thought leader and contributor can be impressive to future employers.

Internships, apprenticeships and graduate programs

List internship, apprenticeship and graduate-program information chronologically in your CV in your 'Work experience' or 'Professional experience' section. If the internship was completed concurrently with other employment, split it out into a separate section. For example, an intern that we hired at people2people was also working part-time for a large insurance company. She took four weeks' annual leave to complete the internship as part of her university degree to further her ambitions within human resources. To avoid interrupting the cohesive nature of her professional experience section on her CV, I would recommend listing this internship under its own section at the back of her CV or, if relevant to the job, right at the front.

Portfolio or work examples

Providing examples of work that you have produced is a great way to showcase to an employer what you are capable of. This is particularly relevant for professionals who work in creative, design, marketing or research fields. Even if you work outside of these areas, you may be able to provide a link or attachment which outlines a particular program, project or idea that you have been instrumental in developing. You can provide a link to a website with your full portfolio, which is recommended for marketing professionals, or you can provide direct links to content in your CV. Here are some work examples that you might like to reference in your CV:

- News articles
- Websites
- Academic research
- Designs
- Marketing campaigns
- Videos

- Social media posts
- Projects
- Books
- Magazines
- Annual reports
- Collateral

If you are preparing a marketing portfolio, think of it like a pseudo-resume where you can include your name, contact details, brief work history, six to eight work examples, awards and a 'call to action'. The way it is presented is just as important as the content as it shows your visual and design capabilities, which are key to many creative positions. An excellent academic portfolio should include similar sections as well as scholarly publications, contributions, collaborations and grants that you've been awarded. Some of the best websites that you can use to build an online portfolio are listed in the 'Useful websites' section at the back of this book.

Media articles

Have you been quoted in the media, or mentioned as part of a story? Where relevant, you can include this information in your CV too. When I'm working with executive candidates with a public profile or professional sports people in preparing their CV, I like to include relevant media articles which illustrate the depth of their experience and success. It might be a press release about their drafting to a football team, a media article about their latest on-field performance or a mention of a sport record that they've broken. For executive candidates, it might be how their organisation was awarded first place on a 'Best places to work' list, or an article where they have commented in the news about a new trend emerging.

Using verified third-party endorsements can showcase to an employer the quality of your thought leadership, experience and achievements. Even if you're a recent graduate, you may have featured positively in articles published by a university alumni organisation, or been listed in the media for a sporting, academic or community achievement. You may have been quoted giving your opinion on a topic and shown thought leadership on climate change, human rights or business trends. Whatever the media article is about, ensure that it is relevant to the job that you're applying to and builds a positive picture of your knowledge, work ethic, experience and attitude to particular issues. Create a 'Media' section towards the back of your CV and provide up to eight media articles of relevance.

Sport, art and extracurricular activities

Showcasing extracurricular activities, where relevant to the position, can highlight your level of commitment, loyalty, passion, teamwork and tenacity to an employer. These can include sport, art and other interests. It shows a wholeness to your personality and a level of balance. As an example, when we hire graduate recruiters at people2people, we look for a pattern of commitment, loyalty and achievement in extracurricular activities, studies or work experience. We seek out interpersonal skills that are evidenced by long-lasting relationships and teamwork. These qualities are more important to us than which degree the candidate has completed.

Volunteer, charity and community work

Volunteer, charity and community work are all relevant to a prospective employer. They show your willingness to learn something new, exposure to various environments and, in many cases, your support of a great cause. Provide some context to your involvement by communicating what the organisation does and how you are involved. You may also volunteer your time for particular projects that can increase your employability.

> **Reflection**
>
> Many years ago, I was asked by a fresh marketing graduate, 'How do I get experience in marketing if I have no marketing experience?' He felt that every job he had applied for had knocked him back because he didn't have any experience. He decided to volunteer his time to build up his marketing experience and created his own side project. He created a LinkedIn group and called it something like 'Melbourne Marketing Professionals'. He went about inviting

members to join and share their ideas about marketing in Melbourne, providing support to the community. He then expanded this network across to other social media platforms. He used his marketing skills to create and post quality content and build up a community of followers. When he applied for his next job, he impressed the prospective employer not only with his community focus but also his skills in digital content management and in building social media audiences. He had given himself a huge advantage when applying for jobs and was quickly employed in marketing.

Endorsements

Including a quote from a previous manager, client or contact of yours that you've been accountable to in the past can be included alongside your referee details. This might say something about what it's like to work with you or your work ethic. Be sure to gain permission to use the quote from the person who gave it. This is not an essential section on your CV but can be a nice touch if the quote is concise, relevant and complimentary.

☕ Coffee break

We've looked at the first page of your CV, the most important opportunity to capture an employer's interest. We've explored your Employee Value Proposition in detail and how we can communicate this through a great tagline or title, profile summary or objective, career overview, highlights section and snapshot of key skills, systems, languages, industries, certifications and memberships. We've shown how to communicate your work history, responsibilities and achievements on your CV for maximum impact and how to back this up with referees and optional sections. Before we move on to cover letters, let's explore tone and formatting in Chapter 7 and, most importantly, how to make your CV stand out from the rest.

Chapter 7

Make yourself stand out

- Tailor your CV and finalise design, tone and formatting.
- Address gaps, temp work, concurrent careers and promotions.
- Position yourself for a career or industry change.

'The world says fit in; the universe says stand out.'

~ Matshona Dhliwayo

Now that you have included the key components of your CV, it is time to look at tone, formatting and design. We will also address common questions and concerns when preparing your CV, such as how to position yourself for a career or industry change and how to avoid discrimination in the recruitment process.

What design, tone and formatting should I use in my CV?

A CV is a factual document that is best when cleanly presented, concise and clear. Stick to the facts, highlight the most important information first and use positive, professional language that shows your proactivity and work ethic. Use a crisp font like Arial, Helvetica or Cambria – anything too fancy will be tiring for the reader, and key points and words can get lost in the design. You can add an element to the design that is unique to you and includes some character or colour. Try to use a font and style that is currently trending, but keep it simple, clean and classic. Ultimately, employers want to read about *you* and your achievements and get a feel for your experience.

Here are some other points to consider:

- If you work in a creative field such as graphic design, showcase your design skills in your CV. When doing this, ensure that your CV is still easy to read and contains all of the relevant information. 'Classic and sophisticated' is always better than 'busy and flashy'. Use clear headings for each new section and subheadings for detail. You can use a one- or two-column format for impact.
- Parallelism can also be used to give equal weighting to ideas of importance in your CV. For example, when listing eight key duties for a position, ensure that they are all of similar importance. Be consistent with how you express each element. This can enhance meaning and significance, and ensure balance in your CV.
- Avoid talking about yourself in the third person; for example, 'Jaime is an experienced farmhand'. It is better to write as you would talk, such as, 'I am an experienced farmhand'.
- Keep your CV length to a maximum of four or five pages. If you are struggling to fit information in, give more weight to recent and relevant experience.

Using Microsoft Word and converting to PDF is absolutely fine when creating your CV, but you can also purchase affordable CV templates online. If you do, make sure that the template format and software can be easily edited and re-formatted to move sections around so that you can tailor your CV to specific jobs. LinkedIn also has a complimentary 'Build a resume' section. Go to your LinkedIn profile, click on 'More' and then 'Build a resume'. This is great for applying for jobs at short notice, but producing a document that you can edit offline is ideal.

If you would like to access some free CV templates, scan the QR code here, or visit people2people.com.au.

Format your CV for parsing engines

When you submit your CV to an employer or recruitment agency, it will most commonly be 'parsed' through a scanning software which picks up keywords and information and populates them into a new user file. For example, if your name and contact number is listed, the software will pull that data from your CV and put it into your contact file with your CV attached. If your CV is in a format other than PDF or Microsoft Word, the system can sometimes reject it. To avoid having your CV rejected or missed, ensure that you submit a PDF version of your CV. This also freezes the design and information in the way that you would like it to look and doesn't allow it to get distorted if the reader has a different software version to you. If you are applying to a recruitment agency, submit a Microsoft Word version of your CV too so that they can recommend you for positions and include a cover page with their recommendations to clients. CV parsing engines may also rank you against the job based on keywords listed in your CV. Let's explore the use of keywords further now.

Use keywords for impact and accessibility

When you apply for a job, many applicant management systems (AMS) rank candidates according to keywords included in their CV and provide search functions that can be used to search applications for a job. So, if 'MYOB' and 'accounting' are important keywords for the job, and you have these listed in your CV, then you might be ranked higher than a candidate without these keywords. When hundreds of applications are in play for the one position, this type of technology is often used to prioritise which candidates to call first. Increase your ranking in the list by packing your CV full of relevant keywords.

Similarly, when recruiters and employers search CV databases, such as those which exist at the back end of SEEK, Indeed and Monster, they will use keywords to find the right people. Keywords include systems, industries, skills, companies, locations and titles. It makes sense, then, to have the right keywords listed throughout your CV. Think about what employers will look for and which keywords they will use when looking to fill the type of position that you want.

> **Case study**
>
> Xander is a recruiter. He is looking for legal secretaries who might like to work for his client, a top-tier law firm. He logs onto his company's candidate database and types in the keywords 'legal secretary'. From experience he knows that similar candidates may also be called 'legal assistant' or 'paralegal', so he uses these search terms too. Taking his search even further, he types in the keyword search terms 'Executive Assistant AND Law Firm', 'Personal Assistant AND Legal' and 'Team Assistant AND Law'. All of these searches produce possible candidates, and Xander identifies the first candidate that he would like to speak with. She has included several of these keywords on her CV and she was easy to find; in fact, she came up in several of his searches. Xander picks up the phone and calls her. 'Hello Amanda…'

Xander is a good recruiter; he's very thorough in his approach. But imagine if he had used only one of those keywords in his search? If it wasn't included in Amanda's CV, she would have been missed altogether. Think of all of the keywords that might be used to search for candidates for the position that you want, and then include them in your CV.

Do I need more than one version of my CV?

Having a base template of your CV and a tailored version for each job is a great idea. The changes might be subtle but could be the difference between being found and interviewed, or not. You could also create template versions of your CV for the different job types that you might apply for. For example, if you're open to applying for a personal trainer job but also for gym customer service, then you might have a slightly different CV for each. Emphasise keywords, experience and skills that relate to the job and make yourself stand out. Make sure that all versions of your CV match up to social media profiles, including your LinkedIn profile, and ensure that each can be backed up by a referee. When the recruiter or employer receives your CV and looks you up online, they need to see consistency and be confident that they are receiving a true and honest account of who you are.

How do I address gaps in my CV?

Whether it's parental leave, unemployment, travel, study or caring for family members, there are many reasons why you might have a gap on your CV. Rather than leaving it blank between positions, try to list the reason for the break and what you did to fill the time. This helps the employer to understand more about your experience to date; but of course, limit personal information to that which you feel comfortable providing.

For example, if you were unemployed for a period of time during which you renovated a house, completed a short course, undertook caring duties or volunteered at a local animal rescue shelter, then list that in your CV. This is more impactful than just listing 'unemployed'. For travel, perhaps list the dates of travel and even where you travelled to. Employers can see travel as an advantage – it can be enriching, educational and provide a huge learning opportunity. It can develop independence, organisational skills, relationship-building skills and problem-solving skills. You might even find some common ground with your interviewer around favourite destinations travelled.

With the above explanations, put them chronologically in your CV in order within your 'Work experience' or 'Professional experience' section. This is so that when an employer is reading through your work experience, they don't have to flick to another page to find out where you were for the time between jobs.

Should I indicate full- or part-time employment?

If you work part-time or full-time, it is completely up to you whether you list it on your CV. You have still been completing the job and getting results, whether you do this part-time or full-time is largely irrelevant. My advice here is intended to reduce unconscious bias and discrimination that a lot of candidates – and particularly return-to-work parents, both male and female – face during the recruitment process. Attitudes to part-time workers are improving, but we still have a long way to go.

> **Reflection**
>
> When I returned to work after having twin boys, I worked part-time, but I always avoided making this publicly known. Even though my employer was incredibly supportive, I was concerned about public perception. After 14 years in recruitment, I had heard enough passing comments like, 'You can't do that job part-time', or 'She's part-time, she's not career-focussed'.
>
> Despite my part-time status, the business that I manage, people2people Recruitment Victoria, has thrived. I've been supported by some very talented people and have an amazing team. I'm also lucky to work with an employer who has always championed results, not hours.
>
> Several of the most successful part-time consultants and managers in the recruitment industry work for people2people, and that is because of a deeply supportive culture. They lead multimillion-dollar desks and teams, and are efficient, effective and inspiring.

I'm pleased to see the growing trend of employers who recognise the value of part-time employees, and who provide flexibility and avoid discrimination in their recruitment and internal career development processes.

The information that you list in your CV can be used fairly or to fuel unconscious bias. Think carefully about what information you would like to include in your CV to ensure that you are given the best opportunity to be invited in for an interview.

Format your CV to avoid unlawful discrimination

In Australia it is unlawful to discriminate against candidates on the basis of age, race, disability, gender, sexual orientation and other personal characteristics. The US, Europe and the UK also have discrimination protections in place for employees. In recruitment processes, the focus should be on the person's experience, skills and ability to do the job. As a candidate applying for jobs, you shouldn't have to worry about unlawful discrimination, but sadly it does still happen. Often this is in the form of unconscious bias. A huge body of research, including the research set out in 'The origins of social categorisation' by Liberman, Woodward and Kinzler, supports the theory that people have a tendency to categorise groups unknowingly and that this behaviour is ingrained from childhood. This can lead to interviewers discriminating based on characteristics not relevant to the job.

You can help reduce the likelihood of unlawful discrimination by only providing information on your CV that is relevant to the job. Leave out information such as your date of birth, age, marital status, race, religion, place of birth and appearance. If you are worried about age discrimination, consider only listing professional experience and education from the last 15 to 20 years of your career. If you are asked questions about any of these areas during a phone screen or interview, you are not obliged to answer. Questions like, 'Are you planning on having kids?', 'Are you married?' or 'What religion do you follow?' are inappropriate and not relevant to the job. Before applying for jobs or interviewing, protect yourself by being clear about what information you are prepared to share and what you would like to keep private.

How do I list temporary and contract work?

Temporary and contract work can be an excellent way to build your experience and skills, discover new environments and enjoy flexibility. However, if you list all of your temporary and contract work individually on your CV without an overarching heading, it can look a bit as if you have been jumping about between permanent jobs. Instead, include a heading such as 'Temporary and Contract Positions' and list all of the positions underneath. You can also include the reason for the contract, such as 'Maternity-leave cover', 'Peak period cover' or 'Project-based contract', as well as whether it was extended. For example, you might say 'Maternity-leave cover (initially 12 months, extended an additional eight months)'.

If you work in a job where contracting is very common, such as IT project management, graphic design or television production, you may like to use the overarching heading format above or list a name for your own company. You can then go on to list the assignments that you have completed under this company.

How do I show promotions within organisations?

You've been promoted – fantastic. You'll want to show this prominently on your CV. But how do you do this without making your CV appear 'jumpy'? At first glance, when you list multiple positions and multiple titles with the one company, it can look like you've been hopping around from job to job, when in fact the opposite is true. Tie this experience up nicely with a clear heading that shows your full employment with the company and the true extent of your tenure.

Here is an example:

Company name   February 2015 to present
www.companyname.com
[Description of the company... 2–3 sentences]

Position A Title   March 2019 to present
Key responsibilities:
[List 8–10]

Key achievements:
[List 2–3]

Position B Title   October 2017 to March 2019
Key responsibilities:
[List 8–10]

Key achievements:
[List 2–3]

Position C Title   February 2015 to September 2017
Key responsibilities:
[List 8–10]

Key achievements:
[List 2–3]

Providing an overarching heading above your promotions makes it clear to a prospective employer that you've had good tenure, loyalty, progression and achievement throughout your employment with the company.

What if I've had two careers concurrently?

Employers are most interested in experience relevant to the job that you're applying for, so always list that first. Let's say you're a professional footballer but also commenced your coaching career while playing. You might have started off with your local football club, then moved into a more senior position, all while playing football.

If you're applying for a coaching position, then the best way to highlight both careers in your CV is to discuss them in separate sections. You can have a section for 'AFL Playing Career' and a section for 'Football Coaching'. Then list all of the relevant experience under each. This is much easier to read and also helps remove the temptation for the prospective employer to see you as 'just a football player'. This concept can be applied to career or job changes too.

> **Case study**
>
> Ranjit is applying for a Social Media Coordinator position. He's currently working at a restaurant in the kitchen, but on the side he's been managing the social media pages for a local community organisation. He's been able to build the Facebook and Instagram audiences from a few hundred followers to over 5000 per page. Even though it's a volunteer position, it's still some of the most relevant experience that he holds in relation to the Social Media Coordinator position.

In this example, Ranjit would list his social media experience first on his CV under a heading called 'Marketing Experience' or 'Social Media Experience'. He would list all of the projects and positions that he's held, whether volunteer or not, in relation to marketing. He would then have a separate heading for 'Additional Employment' and list his restaurant job there.

How can I position myself for a career or industry change?

The key to positioning yourself for a career or industry change on your CV is to focus on transferable skills, your EVP and using keywords to engage the reader. Write down all of the skills required for the new job you are pursuing and all of the skills that you currently have. Give yourself credit for skills that you might have utilised less but have nonetheless developed. You will still need to obtain any specific qualifications and certifications that are required before applying for jobs in a new career, but additionally market your transferable skills effectively. Below are some examples of overlapping skills between different positions.

Current position	Career-change position
Nurse: In-depth knowledge and understanding of pharmaceutical medicines Excellent relationship-development skills obtained through quality patient care Strong administrative and organisational skills used to triage patients, update records and communicate with all departments via email and phone	**Account Manager – Pharmaceuticals:** In-depth knowledge and understanding of pharmaceutical medicines Relationship and business development Strong administrative and organisational skills
Graduate Accountant: Preparing presentations for the CFO to present to the board Coordinating delivery of auditing documents onsite First point of contact for the accounting department and providing financial data to the marketing department regarding social media campaigns	**Marketing Coordinator:** Preparing presentations for sales pitches to marketing departments Coordinating promotional items for events Managing communication and social media pages
Dancer: Attending opening night functions and promoting the dance company's work and philanthropic opportunities Collaborating with team members on dance sequences and choreography projects Using organisational skills to coordinate travel requirements and preparation for each performance	**Fundraising Coordinator:** Attending networking events and promoting the charity to prospective donors Collaborating with team members on fundraising projects Using organisational skills to coordinate events and campaigns

When listing information under each position in your CV, emphasise key duties and achievements that are most relevant to the job that you are applying for. Include a 'Key Skills' section and note all of your transferable skills that address the key selection criteria and market you effectively for the role. Include a tagline or title that states the new career that you are pursuing under your name, and list key highlights below. For example:

Joseph Bungala
Marketing Coordinator
SEO | SEM | ABL | BTL | Collateral | Copywriting | Design Coordination | Video Production | Social Media | Public Relations | UX Design

Your ultimate goal is for the prospective employer to call you and to ask more. This gives you the opportunity to discuss the career change and what you could bring to the position. Sometimes a fresh perspective is welcomed over linear progression.

> **Case study**
>
> Ida is applying for a Finance Manager position at a large medical device company. She has no industry experience and thinks that this will work against her. When the employer receives Ida's CV and sees that she has a lot of experience working within logistics and insurance, they are immediately excited by the fresh perspective that she might be able to bring to the job. Even though many other candidates have worked in healthcare and medical devices before, Ida is an attractive candidate because of the new ideas and knowledge that she can offer. She is immediately called by the employer to discuss her application further.

When career-changing, your previous career and experience can actually be an advantage and add a lot of value to an organisation. You may need to be more active and vocal during your job search in order to be considered, but once you're noticed, many employers will want to know more.

Summarising your CV in resume format

If you need a resume rather than a CV, here are some suggestions for formatting it. A resume is commonly used in the US, Canada and parts of Europe, and should be no more than two pages. It is a summary of your CV. Here are the key sections to include:

- Contact details and social media handles
- Summary or highlights
- Professional experience – positions, companies, dates of employment
- Education
- Skills, languages, systems, industries where relevant.

Your resume is a marketing document that promotes you with the goal of getting you an interview. If you are succinct in articulating your EVP and key selling points, you can show a prospective employer how you can add value.

Finalising and updating your CV

It may sound obvious, but the importance of proofreading your CV can't be overstated. A 2021 Adzuna study of 40,000 CVs submitted as part of real job applications showed that 67% of the CVs submitted contained at least one spelling error, and more than half had four or more spelling mistakes. So it pays to hand your CV to a friend or two, or a professional contact, and ask for their feedback and advice. The most common errors recruiters see on submitted CVs are random capitals, ampersands, spelling and grammatical errors, and inconsistencies in format, spacing and punctuation. If in doubt, look it up, and show attention to detail, design and care in your CV.

Tailor your CV to the job that you are applying for each time, highlighting any key selection criteria and keywords. Alter the order and prominence of sections in your CV to showcase those most applicable to the job, and reconcile them with your social media profiles.

Once you have built your CV, update it as you move through your career, while the content is fresh in your mind.

> ### ☕ Coffee break
>
> Whether it's putting together a personal website, application video or creative design, there are several ways you can make your job application stand out. I've heard of job seekers taking out Google advertisements to promote themselves, advertising on billboards or building their CV out of LEGO. Whatever approach you take, ensure that you think of the employer's recruitment process and what will impress them. My top creative pick for standing out is to submit a video along with your CV, which we'll talk about further in Chapter 8.

In this chapter, we've discussed how to stand out when putting your CV together. You can consider design, tone and formatting, and use keywords for impact and accessibility. We've looked at how to tailor your CV for each job and reconcile it with your social media profiles. You can also address gaps, promotions and career changes proactively, and display temp and contract work well. Limiting the information you choose to provide in your CV can also help to avoid unlawful discrimination. Lastly, we've looked at how to summarise your CV into resume format and how to keep it updated along the way. Before we look at job-search techniques, let's discuss cover letters and how to get that call for an interview.

Chapter 8

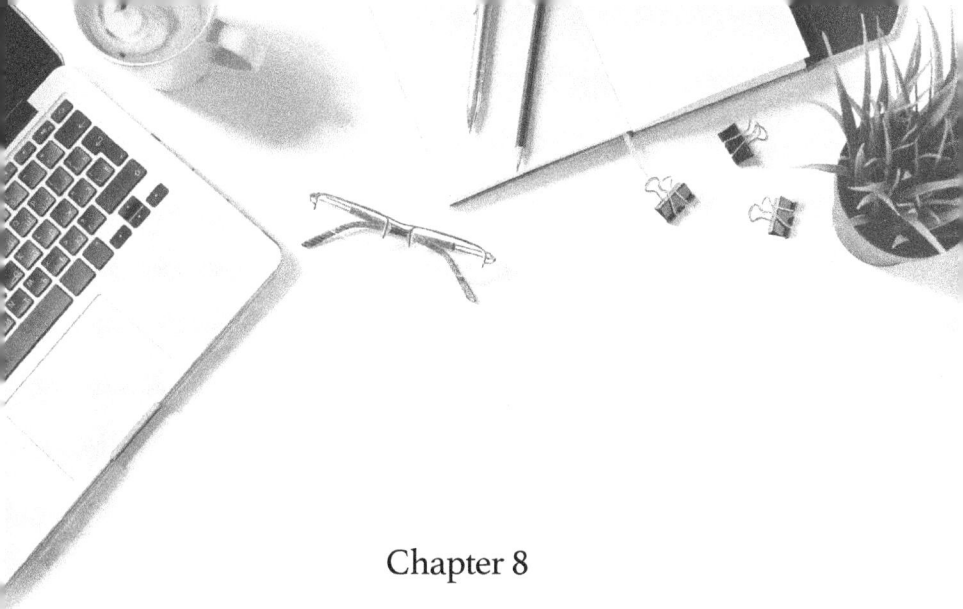

Cover letters with impact

- Tailor your cover letter for each job and address key selection criteria.
- Highlight values, achievements, experience, education and skills.
- Stand out by adapting your cover letter into an application video.

A well-written cover letter can be the cherry on top that lands you an interview for the job that you are really interested in. You can address key selection criteria, highlight achievements, skills and experience, and show a prospective employer why you are the right candidate for the job. A cover letter is a great place to convey enthusiasm, confidence and competence, and inspire the recruiter or employer to call you. You may even want to expand this concept to a video. Your writing or speaking style says a lot about your work ethic, attitude and professionalism, and can really help you stand out. Let's explore the different elements of writing an excellent cover letter.

Should I submit a cover letter?

For some job applications, a cover letter is clearly requested. Always take the time to write one in these situations and show the employer that you've understood the job application requirements. But what if a cover letter isn't requested? Should you submit one then? The answer depends on several factors. First, make sure that you have time to write it properly. A sloppy cover letter is far worse than not submitting one at all. Second, don't delay your application more than a day to get your cover letter in. If it's Monday and you'll have to wait until the weekend to write it, you may have missed the boat on the job opportunity by then. In these instances, it's better to tailor and submit your CV or resume straight away, then come back at a later date to write the cover letter. You can send it to the employer separately or call and advise that you'd like to provide some more information. It gives you a great reason to call, shows your proactivity and allows you to be noticed by the recruiter. They will understand and appreciate your sense of urgency in getting your CV or resume in. The fact that you're prepared to follow up and provide more detail shows that you are really committed, thorough and interested in the opportunity.

Of course, submitting your cover letter upfront with your CV or resume is even better. You can always prepare a template cover letter that can be changed and adapted for each job. This will cut down the time it takes to prepare each one. Frustratingly, research tells us that only a small percentage of cover letters are actually read, but when they are reviewed, they can be a huge influencing factor. Let's look at what to include and how to motivate an employer to call you for an interview.

Cover letter format

The most traditional of cover letters follow a modern business-letter-writing style derived from *ars dictaminis*, an early stylised type of letter writing which was formalised in Italy in the 12th century.

To show respect for tradition, include the following elements in your cover letter:

Your name
Your address or suburb
Your phone number
Your email

Date

Recipient's name
Title
Company
Address
Email address

Dear (person's name),

Re: Title of position you are applying for

Body of letter

Sincerely (or another formal sign off),

Your signature

Your name
Mobile number
Email address

You can use the formal greeting of 'Dear…', or for relaxed company environments you can use the greeting 'Hi…'. Avoid 'To whom it may concern' as it is outdated. Align the sender, date and recipient sections fully left or fully right – either is appropriate. Having a clear subject heading bold and centred in your cover letter after the greeting line can help focus the reader on the reason for your contact. Keep your tone professional, friendly, respectful and positive, and be sure to tailor your information specifically to the job.

Cover letter content

The first step in preparing content for your cover letter is to review the job advertisement or job description thoroughly in advance. Highlight key selection criteria and other areas of importance. Pay special attention to duties, objectives, values and the skills required for the job. Addressing these throughout your cover letter will be key to impressing an employer. Plan the content of your paragraphs first by deciding which key selection criteria you are going to focus on and how you will address them. Include examples from your work history that demonstrate achievements, skills and capabilities that address each job requirement. Here is an example:

ABC Banking Corporation is recruiting for a retail banker position. The list of key selection criteria includes excellent interpersonal and communication skills, knowledge of banking or financial procedures and strong attention to detail. The list of responsibilities for the position includes administrative tasks, customer service and handling customer enquiries. Farah is applying for this position and she uses the following paragraph in her cover letter:

'With three years' experience in retail customer service, I have enjoyed assisting customers, problem-solving and communicating effectively at all times. Stock control within the store required a high level of attention to detail, and I was regularly appointed to reconcile inventory records, cash register amounts and supplier invoices. I used strong administrative skills to answer customer emails, liaise with company departments and assist with roster preparation and scheduling.'

While it is clear that Farah doesn't have any banking experience, she has impressed in her cover letter by focussing on transferable skills.

Keep your cover letter to a maximum of two pages, with one page the preferred length. You should include four or five paragraphs that address different aspects of the job and convince an employer why they should call you.

Emphasise achievements

Perhaps you've improved customer experience in the past, worked really well in a team or delivered above expectations? Whatever your achievements are, try to emphasise these in your cover letter by using them in response to key selection criteria. For example, if one of the criteria is excellent budget management skills, then you might say:

> 'As General Manager of XYZ Company, I was able to navigate the business through challenging times during the COVID-19 lockdowns. I used budget management and cost-control measures to reduce our cost base and negotiate with suppliers for relief and support. In one instance, pausing a $180K contract for six months delivered over $90K worth of relief when we needed it most.'

Incorporate employer values

Pay attention to the values that an employer lists on their website or within a job description. These are often central to the organisation's hiring processes and are particularly dear to human resources (HR) professionals and line managers, who can be at the frontline of recruitment decision-making. Here is an example of where a candidate has addressed values well in their cover letter:

> *XYZ Corporation is recruiting for a Fibre Optics Technician and their values are innovation, accountability, care, teamwork and excellence. Scott writes a cover letter addressing other key selection criteria and also addresses some of the company's values in the following paragraph:*
>
> 'Care, excellence and accountability have been central to previous fibre optics technician positions that I have worked in, which

aligns well with XYZ Corporation's values. I have always felt accountable to customers in restoring their telecommunications and internet services quickly, allowing them to work, learn, enjoy entertainment and communicate with family and friends. Working as part of a team of technicians, I have collaborated to come up with new and innovative technical solutions that can achieve these goals more efficiently.'

Clarify parts of your CV or resume

Your cover letter is a great place to elaborate on key information in your CV or resume, as well as specific situations like gaps in your CV, periods of leave or career changes. It allows you to explain your circumstances more fully and clear up any confusion. Your personal information is just that though; only reveal what you feel comfortable discussing, and only do so if it may increase your chances of securing an interview. Here are three examples:

Visa status

'I currently hold a Working Holiday Visa (417) and have already completed 88 days' worth of regional work, qualifying for my second-year visa. I am available for up to six months' work with the one employer and am ready to take on long-term temporary and contract positions.'

Return to work after parental leave

'Finishing up with XYZ company in December 2019, I took one year of paternity leave to care for my young son. I am now ready to return to my career in a full-time capacity in an innovative, forward-thinking organisation where teamwork is valued.'

Moving locations

'After moving to Brisbane for my partner's defence-force job, I took on temp and contract work between 2018 and 2020. This provided me with excellent exposure to new ideas, environments, work practices and cultures. We have now moved permanently back to Adelaide, where I look forward to engaging in permanent, long-term employment with a supportive and culturally diverse organisation.'

Demonstrate research

Showing a prospective employer that you've taken the time to research their company online is a great way to impress. You could review their annual report, news section, careers website or 'about us' page and incorporate a nod to relevant information in your cover letter. Here's an example for a Communications Manager position:

'ABC Company's recent merger with XYZ company is an exciting move. I have written internal communications during a similar process at DEF company. If appointed, I would enjoy assisting ABC company with their merger communications and look to support all employees and stakeholders with clear, consistent information.'

Express enthusiasm

Employers often seek positive, 'can do' attitudes, and prospective employees who are excited about what their company does and their vision for the future. You can use your cover letter to convey interest and enthusiasm. Here's an example for a solar business:

'I am passionate about environmental sustainability and renewable energy. If given the opportunity to join ABC Solar Company, I look forward to helping contribute to a greener future for all.'

Show why you're the right candidate for the job

By addressing key selection criteria in each paragraph, you can show a prospective employer why you're the right candidate for the job.

You can also finish your cover letter with a clear indication of why they should hire you. For example, for an architect position with a property developer where the key criteria are excellent design skills, stakeholder management and attention to detail, you might say:

> 'In this position I would bring six years' experience in architecture, and a passion for design and attention to detail. If appointed, I look forward to an opportunity to engage with key stakeholders, collaborate on sustainable building designs and uphold ABC Company's reputation as a market-leading property developer.'

Finish with a call to action

A 'call to action' is a phrase that tells the reader what the next steps are and how to go about them. In a cover-letter situation, this simply means encouraging the employer to call you. After your final paragraph, which summarises why you are the right candidate for the job, end with a call to action, a formal sign-off and your contact details. Here's what this might look like:

> 'Thank you for taking time to review my application. I look forward to hearing from you soon.'

Or:

> 'If you require any further information, please don't hesitate to reach out. I look forward to hearing from you.'

Or:

> 'Thank you for your time. I look forward to hearing from you to discuss this further and can be contacted on the mobile number below.'

Followed by a formal sign-off:

> 'Sincerely,'

Or:

> 'Kind regards,'

Or:

> 'Regards,'

Then sign your name or provide an electronic signature. Add your full printed name, phone number and email address. Having contact details at the start *and* end of your cover letter makes it easy for the employer to pick up the phone and call you.

If you would like to access a free cover letter template, scan the QR code here, or visit people2people.com.au.

Record a video cover letter

In the future I expect video cover letters to be standard, but for now you can record one to really stand out. You can outline who you are, why you are interested in the position and what you can bring to the role. I recommend keeping your video to a maximum of 60 seconds. An employer can appreciate a short video, but anything longer might have them clicking 'next'. Remember, your goal is for the employer to call you for an interview. Here is the video format that I recommend:

Format

- Explanation of who you are
- What experience, skills and qualifications you bring
- Why you're interested in the job
- How you can add value
- Why they should select you
- How they can contact you

Template

'Hi (name of hiring person), my name is (your name). I'm a (title of profession) with (number of years') experience. I have (a), (b), (c) skills and a (name of qualification/s). I like (say something about their company or industry). I bring (skill/experience) to the job and, if appointed, look forward to assisting with (d). With (e), (f) and (g) I believe I could help (name of company) achieve its goals of (h), underpinned by the values of (list the company's values). If you would like to discuss further, please contact me on (mobile number) or (email).'

Example

'Hi Louisa, my name is Owen. I'm a pool lifeguard with two years' experience. I have first aid, CPR and emergency procedures skills and a Bachelor of Physical Education. I like the community focus that Neighbourhood Swimming Pool has and how you have engaged your guests with events, activities and links to local festivals. I bring strong teamwork, diligence and physical capability to the job of lifeguard. If appointed, I look forward to helping keep Neighbourhood Swimming Pool's guests safe, happy and cared for. With knowledge of advanced water rescues, a passion for customer service and an eye for detail, I believe I could help Neighbourhood Swimming Pool support and engage the community, underpinned by the values of teamwork, safety, service and excellence. If you would like to discuss further, please contact me on 0000 000 000 or owensemail@email.com.au.'

When recording your video, speak into the camera as if you are having a conversation with another person, and try to move your hands and body naturally. Choose a good background with quality lighting and dress professionally to appear on screen, the same as you would for an interview. Be friendly, genuine and honest about your interest and what you can offer. As daunting as appearing on video might be, if you can overcome your nerves to speak on camera, it could be just the edge you need to get your foot in the door.

☕ Coffee break

In summary, take the time to prepare a quality cover letter and make yourself really stand out. Use a formal business-letter format and positive, professional language. You can also be complimentary about the organisation and demonstrate the research you've undertaken about the company. Address key selection criteria, highlight achievements, incorporate values and show your enthusiasm. Demonstrate the skills and experience you have that are relevant to the job. You can also take time to explain any parts of your CV or resume that require elaboration or expand on unusual situations affecting you. A well-written cover letter can really make you stand out and help you get an interview for the job that *you* want. Better still, create a video version of your cover letter and show that you are truly unique. The right approach to job searching can also make a huge difference in whether you get an interview or not. Let's explore this now in Chapter 9.

Part IV
Search and apply

Chapter 9

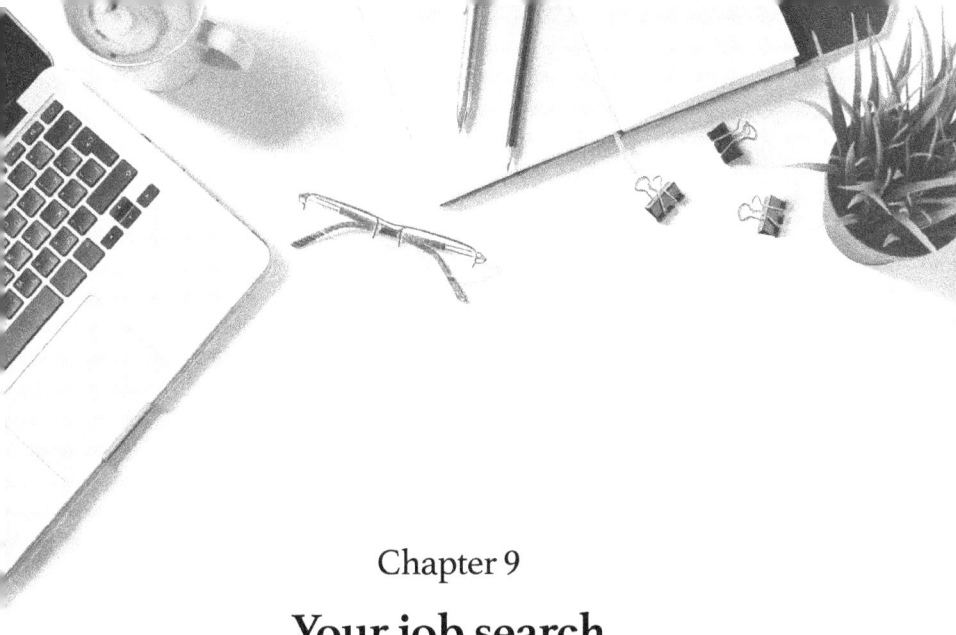

Your job search

- Look in all the right places for your job search.
- Stand out by tailoring your applications and following up.
- Network, build relationships and work with a specialist recruiter.

You've developed your EVP, prepared your CV and have a template cover letter ready to go. Your online profiles are up to date, and your professional social media accounts are looking fantastic. With all of this preparation, you are well on your way to applying for the job that you *really* want. Now, you'll need to plan your job search like a sales campaign and align it with your career goals. Decide where to look, register with specialist recruitment agencies and set up your job board profiles. Before pressing 'submit' on your job application, you'll want to tailor your CV to the job and update your cover letter. You may encounter different application processes, types of software, pre-interview assessments and questions. To stand out, you'll want to follow up your job application professionally and get the timing right. Let's explore these steps now and look at how to increase your chances of getting an interview.

Your successful job-search strategy

You've planned your career goals, decided what you are looking for in an employer and developed your EVP. It's time to prepare your job-search plan. Here are my top ten tips for a successful job search that increases your chances of securing an interview.

1. Make space

Finding the right job requires time and space. Set up a dedicated area in your house where you can search for job opportunities comfortably and make notes and calls. Ask for support from family members by letting them know that you are looking for a new position. You'll need time to search, tailor your CV and cover letters, and follow up your applications. It's better to select positions carefully and decide which opportunities you would like to put your time into. A rushed application can stay on file with a company or recruitment agency for a long period of time, so it's worth getting it right upfront and making a great first impression.

2. Set a goal

Some job seekers are only passively looking, and others are very active. If you're a passive job seeker, you may only want to apply for a job here and there, but if active you'll need a much higher target. TalentWorks research shows that you have an 8.3% chance of getting an interview from a single job application. That means on average you will need to submit at least 12 job applications to get an interview. Following the advice in this book will help you lower that number, but it's still a great idea to set yourself a goal in terms of the number of jobs you would like to apply for each week or month.

Expect to invest at least 30 minutes of searching and research time before deciding on a position you would like to apply for. Then add at least another 30 minutes to tailor your CV and cover letter from your templated versions. If you're currently working full-time, a goal of one to three applications per week might be realistic, while this number could be higher if you're unemployed, such as five to ten applications per week. This can change depending on whether your profession is oversupplied with candidates and how frequently vacancies come up. For example, executive positions are often hotly contested and don't come up as frequently as frontline positions. With jobs that require niche skills that are 'in demand', you may only need to apply for a few jobs to get an interview if you have the required experience. On the flip side, customer service and administration jobs are often oversupplied with candidates, meaning that there are many more applicants than jobs. For these positions, it's best to apply for a higher number of jobs to increase your chances of success.

Less is often more, though, in a job-search scenario. The career goals that you set back in Chapter 1 can help inform the type of jobs that you might apply for. A scattergun approach to job searching can be as damaging as not applying at all. Instead, you might choose to reduce the number of jobs that you apply for but increase the quality of your applications. Invest time in well-written cover letters and intelligent follow-up calls where applicable. If you do your research properly you can help to ensure that you're applying for a job that you're really interested in.

3. Use helpful tools for record keeping and follow-up

A good salesperson is organised and always uses a customer relationship management (CRM) system to support their projects and communications. Whether it's a comfortable thought for you or not, sales is exactly what you are doing with your job search. You are selling *you* and what you can offer an employer. Don't worry though: it's a two-way street. Employers will be selling to you as well and trying to gain your interest. Be organised with your job search and set up a data management system. Microsoft Excel or Numbers is perfect, along with document folders to save additional information into. Track the jobs that you are interested in and have applied for, and the status of your applications, as well as contacts, timelines and follow-up activities. Here is an example of the headings you might use:

Job applications tracker

Job title	Company	Company website	Job ad link	Applied date	Files submitted	Contact details	Close date	Status

Note the job title, company name and website. This makes it easier to research the organisation before tailoring your application. Keep a link to the job and download or cut and paste the advert into your own documents folder to refer back to at a later date. This is handy if the advertisement expires or is taken down and you'd like to follow up your application with the right information to hand. You can also use it to prepare for an interview if you progress to this stage. You'll have more information, be better prepared and most likely feel more confident.

As you tailor your CV and cover letters, save your documents in a separate folder for each job. Your file path might be: *Documents/Job Search/Jobs/ABC Job Application*. Save both your CV and cover letter in there. If you are invited in for an interview, you will want to ensure that you are working off the same documents as the recruiter or employer. A well-organised filing system can help with quick recall.

List the contact details of the person responsible for recruiting the position. This might be the recruiter managing the job or a direct line manager. Some positions have a close date, but most will not; if there is one, list it in your spreadsheet. Lastly and most importantly, keep detailed notes of where you are up to in regard to each job. For example:

> 'Application submitted on 01.10.21, follow-up call to recruiter 3.10.21 and phone-screened. Recruiter advised response being reviewed this week and call-backs for interviews next week. Follow up next on 15.10.21.'

You can set calendar reminders to notify you of when to follow up your job applications. Many job boards have phone apps that you can download to track and manage applications too. Being organised and methodical about your job search is key. It's not the candidate that applies that stands out, it's the candidate that applies in a timely fashion with a well-tailored CV, cover letter and intelligent follow-up.

4. Tailor your CV and cover letter

In chapters six through eight we looked at how to tailor your CV and cover letter effectively. Keywords and phrases that spark interest are important, along with relevant experience, skills and education being listed right at the top. According to CareerBuilder, the number-one desire of recruiters and employers is to receive a CV or resume tailored to the job, with 63% rating this as critical. Yet research shows that the majority of job applicants don't tailor their CV or resume. It's an easy and simple way to help yourself stand out. Take the extra 20 to 30 minutes and the results could surprise you.

5. Create profiles on major job boards

Job boards like SEEK, Indeed and Monster give you the ability to create a profile that can be searched for and found by recruiters and employers. On your profile, include a CV or resume that pitches you well to the main jobs that you are planning to apply to. You may be asked to include details of your last or current position, education and skills, as well as industries that you are interested in. They'll also ask for your location and role preferences, such as how far you are happy to travel and minimum salary requirements. The more flexible you are with your criteria, the more likely you are to be called by a recruiter or employer. Be sure to include as much information as possible so that you are found when recruiters search for particular skills, or candidates in a certain location or salary bracket. Switch your profile to 'available' or 'open to opportunities' and allow your CV to be downloaded by recruiters. This increases the chances that you will be considered for and contacted about jobs. Keep your contact details and preferences up to date as your situation changes and help the right opportunities come to you.

6. Make a great follow-up call

Some employers will cringe when I say this, but I guarantee that making a great follow-up call will help you stand out. It allows you to briefly showcase your experience, have your CV noticed for all the right reasons and understand where the recruiter is up to in the process. A good recruiter will be able to phone-screen you and assess your suitability on the spot. Be sensitive as to whether the person you are calling can actually take your call. Internal recruiters sometimes manage 30 to 50 jobs simultaneously and that means they are responsible for communicating with thousands of potential candidates. Realistically, they won't always be able to take your call. Agency recruiters are more likely to be available to do so, handling about 5 to 15 jobs simultaneously. There are often multiple recruiters across the same job, so you may speak to one of several recruiters within the agency, not just the consultant listed on the advertisement.

> **Reflection**
>
> When recruiting, I absolutely love it when candidates call me. It saves hours of work and helps me to quickly identify proactive, engaged and intelligent candidates. I can do an immediate assessment against

the job and give honest feedback in the moment. It allows me to advise candidates if they are a strong prospect for the position, or if the employer is seeking a specific skill or type of experience. I can help candidates understand how far the job is from their home and what visa requirements are in place, and update them on where we are up to in the recruitment process. Some of the best candidates I have placed in jobs over the years took the time to call me early in the recruitment process and highlight their strengths.

How you execute this follow-up call is critical. Make the call a day or two *after* your application is sent, so that the recruiter or employer can pull up your details while you are talking to them. Try to be professional, respectful and succinct. 'Hi, I'm calling for a job', or 'Hi Mary, I'm just calling to see if you've had a chance to review my resume?' is not the best approach for a recruiter or employer who has hundreds and possibly thousands of CVs to review. A better approach is to use this three-step formula that incorporates key selling points without being salesy or overt:

1. Introduce yourself, including a couple of key selling points.
2. Advise which job you are calling about.
3. Check whether the employer has received your resume.

Here are a few examples:

> 'Hi Pierce, my name's Larissa; I'm a full stack developer, I'm currently working at XYZ company and I saw that you are looking for a full stack developer. I've applied and I was just following up to check that you'd received my CV okay.'

Or:

> 'Hi Max, my name's Cora; I'm a mechanical engineering graduate and I've just completed my heavy vehicle truck licence. I noticed that you're looking for a graduate service engineer. I've applied and I'm just following up to see if you would like any further information from me.'

This approach is effective because it immediately draws the recruiter's attention to the fact that you have some relevant experience, skills or qualifications, and it also directs them to your CV. By asking the recruiter to look it up, they will either conduct a quick phone-screen with you on the spot or acknowledge that they have received it and will review it later. Now that they have pulled up your file, though, why not have a look at your experience then and there? Remember that recruiters can receive hundreds of applications per job, so even just getting your CV in front of them can really make you stand out. Be sensitive to their time constraints, however, and understand that you may not get through immediately.

If the employer or recruiter says that they've received your CV, thank them for confirming this and be open to a phone-screen. For example: 'Excellent, thank you for confirming. I'm very interested in the position. Is there anything else that you would like to know while you have me on the phone?' If they say no, respectfully leave the conversation there, thank them for their time and advise that you're looking forward to hearing back. If they say yes, then you have likely prompted them to conduct a more thorough phone-screen with you, which is a great outcome.

If specific instructions about the employer's recruitment process and how and when they would like to be contacted are listed, then it is always best to follow these. You may also like to submit an application video to help yourself stand out, as discussed in Chapter 8. This can be a great replacement for a follow-up call, although it doesn't necessarily help the recruiter find your CV. In the absence of strict instructions, a follow-up call is best, and can really help your application to be noticed and spark interest with the recruiter or employer.

7. Timing is everything

A job has a closing date in four weeks' time: that means you've got four weeks to prepare your CV and cover letter, right? Wrong.

You can certainly take this approach, but I can almost guarantee you that you'll be too late. When a position is vacant, that often means that work isn't getting done or someone else is managing the workload – often the manager hiring for the role. This means they are usually highly motivated to get the position filled quickly and ensure that the work is passed back over. Some organisations have closing dates as part of their process, but it doesn't always signify the date that they will start reviewing applications. It can simply represent the last date that candidates will be eligible to apply. Most employers start reviewing applications and interviewing soon after the job is posted. So if you wait four weeks, they might have already interviewed five or six people and progressed to offer stage.

To have the best chance of success, get in early and apply on the first or second day. Review job boards daily during your job search, and if something catches your eye, make time to apply early. Being one of the first applicants means that you are on a much shorter list of applicants, and the chances of your CV being reviewed are very high. Recruiters look through job ad responses daily. On the first day there may only be ten applicants, but by the second or third day there could be over a hundred. When employers engage recruitment agencies for temp and contract positions, they often expect a 'same-day fill'; that is, where the job is filled the same day that it is listed, or very shortly after. Getting in quickly with your application is essential in these situations.

It also pays to be responsive. You've put all of the work into your job application but only check your emails weekly? This scenario could be as disastrous as not having voicemail on your phone. Keep your mobile handy, check communication channels daily and respond as soon as reasonably possible. Make sure that you have an active voicemail service on your mobile phone and avoid voice-to-text or ten-second messages.

Privacy can be an issue if you receive a phone call and are still working for an employer, but ducking out during your lunchbreak can be a great way to tackle this. Email correspondence is common with larger employers, and phone calls are most commonly used by recruitment agency consultants. Email messages can be system-generated, so be sure to check your junk folder too. Even if you've lost interest in the opportunity, it's a good idea to call back anyway and update the recruiter or employer on your status. Recruitment agencies and employers may keep your record on file for future positions, so it helps to develop a good relationship from the beginning.

8. Network and foster relationships

While the vast majority of permanent positions are advertised via job boards, many are filled before they even get advertised. This is particularly true for temporary and contract positions, which are often filled by recruitment agencies with candidates who are already registered, interviewed and qualified. Research suggests that 60% of job vacancies are not actually advertised. Many organisations have requirements to advertise permanent positions either directly or via a recruitment agency, but there are also times when preferred candidates may have been earmarked before this takes place. A great example of where I've observed this scenario is within the sporting industry. It's common for each club to know the coaching, playing and executive staff from other clubs and have an idea in their mind of who they would like to approach for a job. Even though they may advertise as well, it's likely that a solid shortlist has already started to form. It pays to be well connected, visible and known in your industry.

A 2015 survey by hiring influencer Lou Adler found that 42% of active employed candidates and 47% of unemployed candidates found their most recent job via networking. The rate was higher among employed passive candidates, where 62% found their job this way. You can build your credibility and visibility in your industry first and foremost by doing a great job. Second, make sure that your social media profiles are up to date and that you're actively engaged. Finally, get out there and meet people.

You can attend events run by your industry association, chambers of commerce, alumni groups and events companies. You can even network through sport, hobbies, volunteering, charity work and friends and family. You never know who your cousin went to school with and where they might be working now. You can join a committee or council that supports your industry, a school, a charity, local government, the environment or your community. Being well connected and visible is extremely beneficial to your job search. If you become unemployed, you can let certain contacts know of your updated status and what type of positions you are interested in. You can also help connect others to job opportunities when they are in a similar position.

Choose events that people who might be useful to your job search are attending, and be on time or early to make the most of networking opportunities. It can be nerve-racking to approach someone you don't know, but the benefits are huge. The other person might be just as nervous as you are, but once you break the ice it could be the foundation of a long-lasting relationship. Exchange contact details and follow up after the event with an email and a LinkedIn connection request. You could say how you enjoyed meeting them or send a link to an article of interest that you mentioned during your chat.

Networking takes time and is most definitely a two-way street. It can be tempting to be highly targeted and forget about the other person's needs, but take a moment to think about how you can help others and ensure mutual benefit. From time to time your new connections may reach out to you for help and advice. It's important to be responsive and supportive without expecting anything in return. Generosity now may help you in the future, and giving altruistically and supporting others is even better.

9. Work with a specialist recruitment agency

According to government research published in 2016, recruitment agencies in Australia represent AU$11.2 billion of the Australian economy and employ over 93,000 people across 7000 recruitment businesses. In the US the market size is over US$120 billion, according to Statista, and in the UK it's £38.9 billion, according to the Recruitment and Employment Confederation (REC). Recruitment agencies represent millions of employer vacancies per year and provide valuable support to candidates and clients. Many organisations have long-term relationships with recruitment consultants and entrust them with their talent attraction, assessment and recruitment.

Working with a specialist recruiter can be advantageous to your career. By building a relationship early, you can then be considered for opportunities moving forward. In skills-short areas, recruiters will even work with you to build a list of employers that you would like to work with and represent you to each company. This can fast-track you into the interview process and allow you to target companies that you really want to work for.

Choose a recruitment agency that is registered with the World Employment Confederation (WEC), or its member organisations, such as the Recruitment, Consulting and Staffing Association (RCSA) in Australia and New Zealand. These respected industry associations are bound by a code of professional conduct, and work actively to ensure excellence in member standards. They advocate for worker rights and provide leadership in the world of work. If the recruiter you are working with is a member of one of these organisations, you can be confident that they are well trained and professional, and uphold high standards.

10. Protect your mental health

Above all else, protecting your mental health is the most important aspect of your job search. Job searching can be exhausting and deflating at times; it's not fun being rejected or knocked back for opportunities. Remember your EVP though. You are incredibly valuable for the right opportunity, and don't let anyone tell you otherwise. If you've been knocked back, it might not be the right match, but it doesn't mean that there isn't an opportunity out there for you. To reduce the mental impact of job searching, I recommend setting your expectations up to anticipate mixed responses. We previously discussed the job application to interview ratio as around 8 to 10%. Zety reports that of candidates interviewed, only 20% are offered the job. We have discussed many ways to increase your chances, but even the most professional candidates will still experience some level of rejection. Be kind to yourself, take a break when you need it and remember how much you have to offer the right employer.

There may also be times where you don't hear back at all from a job application. It's frustrating and unprofessional, but sadly it does happen. PredictiveHire research showed that candidates who received feedback on their application, whether successful or not, reported 99% satisfaction with their experience. Seventy per cent were also more likely to recommend the company as an employer of choice. Not all employers have clued onto this data or thought enough about the candidate experience. There is plenty of software and artificial intelligence (AI) available to assist employers in updating candidates. After all of the time and effort that you have put into your job application, it's not too much to expect a response. Don't be afraid to pick up the phone and ask for an update if you haven't heard back within a couple of weeks. Be friendly, professional and respectful, and if the job isn't filled then you might just inspire them to look at your CV.

Your health and happiness are more important than getting the perfect job, so if your job search is getting you down, take a break and return when you feel ready.

Where to look

For your job search you can use a combination of job boards, social media sites, company career pages, recruitment and employment service providers, government sites, networking and word-of-mouth referrals. There are mainstream job boards like SEEK, Indeed and LinkedIn in Australia. (Some other international job boards are listed in the 'Useful websites' section at the back of this book.). You can also find job boards owned by industry associations, universities and recruitment agencies.

Recruitment agency job boards provide opportunities across multiple employers. Even better, if you are already registered with the recruitment agency and have been interviewed, then you can flag any jobs of interest with your recruitment consultant. If there is a good match, they can then fast-track you into the client's interview process. Be sure to register with a professional, licensed and accredited recruiter who is a member of the World Employment Confederation (and RCSA in Australia and New Zealand). They will be able to match you to employers based on your work preferences, skills and experience, and can ensure that your pay, workplace rights and work health and safety are looked after.

Social media sites like LinkedIn have job boards and also serve up job advertisements while you're reading other posts. They match these to your profile via a sophisticated algorithm. Following recruitment agencies and in-house talent acquisition managers on social media can also be a great way to become aware of opportunities. They often use visual tiles to advertise positions, and these can include roles that haven't hit the mainstream job boards.

Employers may have career pages or entire websites dedicated to careers and talent acquisition. You can conduct research on the company, understand their benefits and culture, and search for open roles. If you have a target list of organisations that you would like to work for, you can even reach out proactively to register so that your details become searchable on their database. You can connect with talent acquisition managers on social media or, where no in-house talent team exists, you can connect with the manager in the company that hires for your type of profession. You can even ask them for a coffee to pick their brain about industry issues and topics. If you do this, make sure that you are honest and transparent from the outset that you are also in the market for job opportunities.

Employment service providers can also assist in your job search if you have been unemployed for a period of time. They are different to recruitment agencies. Recruitment agencies are engaged by businesses to find the right talent for their organisation and are paid by the organisation to do so. An employment service provider is often government- or charity-funded and works to support unemployed candidates in gaining meaningful employment. They can help you prepare for and look for work, as well as provide access to training. They also often have computers and phones available that you can use to look for work. Additionally, there are some excellent support organisations, such as Fitted for Work, that can help support you in your job search if you are facing challenging situations.

Government websites can also be an excellent resource for job support and opportunities. In Australia you can visit servicesaustralia.gov.au for resources and support, and find job opportunities via the jobactive.gov.au website. If you are living with a disability you can access Disability Employment Services to support your job search, and if you are located in a regional area then the Work Assist program may help. Internationally, look at your local government websites and explore job support and opportunities there.

Diversity recruitment – how does that work? Employers are becoming more aware of freeing themselves from biases related to candidates' age, gender, sexual orientation, race, religion and personal characteristics that are not related to the job at hand. Many organisations now set diversity targets that they seek to achieve to increase the diversity of their workforce. There are often diversity and inclusion policies that underpin these goals. You can provide additional information during your job applications that can help employers identify you as someone who can increase diversity in their workforce. You can also register with specific diversity recruitment agencies and job boards that help organisations to further these goals.

The application process

Each employer has a unique application process that can be as simple as emailing your CV, or as complex as behavioural profiling and video interviewing. The simplest form of submitting your CV and cover letter is via email. It is rarely used these days, however, as applicant tracking systems have become more popular; they save time and provide a better experience for employers and candidates. If you are uploading your CV directly to the employer's website or database, you can expect to see many different interfaces and page formats. Have key details ready such as contact information, your tailored CV, cover letter and referees.

Companies may also use an aggregator or job board where you can upload your resume, which is then forwarded on to the organisation who has advertised the job. By uploading your CV to the job board, you are often added to their online database by default and encouraged to fill out your profile. You will have the option at this point to either accept and fill out the details or make your profile private to hide it from employers. Whether you do this depends on how passive or active you are as a candidate and your privacy preferences.

Applying with LinkedIn is also an option across many job sites, recruitment agency job boards and employer career sites. This method is popular in skills-short areas, allowing candidates to apply without having to prepare a full CV. If you do use this method, you can always follow up later with a full CV to showcase your skills, experience and particular achievements in more detail.

Some employers and recruitment agencies have deployed AI within their application processes, which can pop up in the form of chat bots who learn more about you and submit this information to the recruiter. There are often workflows in place that direct you one way if your answer matches the job and another if it doesn't. This is designed to screen candidates more effectively and provide faster feedback about their application status. There are also a multitude of screening and assessment methods that companies use to determine which candidates to progress through to interview. We will explore these further in Chapter 11.

☕ Coffee break

Making space for your job search and setting goals can help you stay focussed and productive. Using record-keeping tools, getting support from loved ones and looking after your mental health is important too. You can stand out by tailoring your CV and cover letter and making a great follow-up call. Set up your online job board profiles to be found proactively by employers, and work closely with a specialist recruitment agency to increase your chances of success. Networking can open doors, and building solid relationships from the beginning can make a great first impression. You may encounter many different interfaces in your job applications, as well as AI, assessments and screening hurdles. If you get the timing of your job applications right and use a variety of sites and methods to find positions, you'll increase your chances of securing an interview.

In Chapter 10 we explore the experience of working with a professional recruitment agency. We'll look at how they can assist you, what to expect throughout the process and where to go for resources and information.

Chapter 10

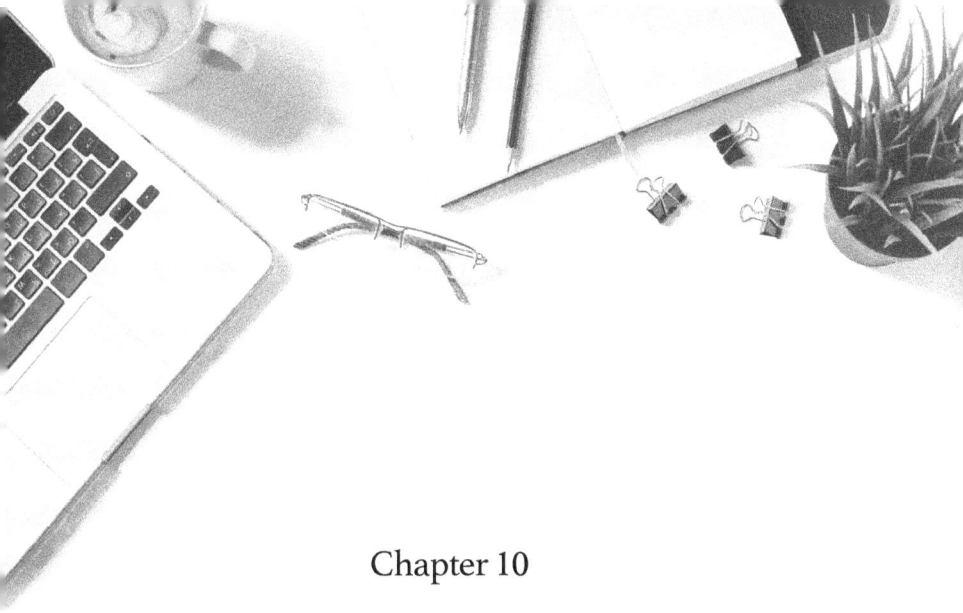

Recruitment agencies

- Partner with a quality recruitment agency.
- Understand what to expect and how agencies work.
- Access hidden job opportunities and specialist market advice.

There are 168 hours in a week. According to Roy Morgan and abc.net.au, on average we humans spend 49 hours sleeping, 35 on socialising and recreation, 28 on domestic work, up to 12 on social media, 5 hours commuting, and 40 hours working. When the average working life is 34% of a waking week, it makes sense to be employed in a job that you actually like.

Many people hire a professional tax accountant to do their tax, a financial adviser for their money matters, a mechanic to fix their car and a doctor to support their health. All of these professionals are experts in their field. Recruitment consultants are also experts in their field and specialise in identifying and engaging with specialist talent. They can also be a great source of support and knowledge for your career direction and progression. They can help accelerate your career, support your employment objectives and provide you with access to additional jobs. You can build long-lasting relationships, provide a detailed brief of what you are looking for and gain professional advice and expertise.

Working as an on-hire employee via a recruitment agency can provide you with additional employment support and opportunities. You can enjoy a variety of work environments, industries and job roles, and upskill in many areas.

> **Case study**
>
> David found his first job as an accountant in the minerals industry through a recruitment agency 25 years ago. He has worked in a range of positions and organisations throughout his career and built strong relationships with a few select professional recruitment agencies. The variety is what he has loved most about agency work. He's been involved in strategy, board reports, banking and finance deals and system implementation that he would never have had exposure to without contracting via a recruitment agency. He's become multiskilled in areas that make him a well-rounded candidate with a lot to offer an employer. Host organisations have commented on David's flexibility, agility and quick learning skills, which he attributes to his exposure to lots of different industries, job roles and environments. He's found the agencies he's dealt with to be friendly, supportive and understanding. He says that they have listened well to his needs and provided him with great work opportunities.

According to the Australian Government Department of Employment, recruitment agencies contribute over $11 billion to the Australian economy each year. Let's look at how recruitment agencies work, how they can support your career goals and what the process is for you as a candidate.

How do recruitment agencies work?

Many organisations around the world partner closely with recruitment agencies to assist in attracting and engaging top talent. The recruitment consultant representing the agency will be briefed in detail by the employer on the organisation's needs and Employer Value Proposition. They will find out about what the organisation does, how big they are, where they operate and what their workplace culture is like. They will gain detail around salaries, awards, pay frequency, induction processes, training, performance reviews, and the organisation's mission, values and future strategy. They will gather information about current and upcoming job opportunities, and which positions the organisation would like to partner with the agency to recruit. Let's look now at some of the benefits that organisations and candidates experience when engaging with a professional recruitment agency.

Specialist expertise

Professional recruitment consultants specialise in particular industries or job roles. They amass niche expertise in understanding candidate profiles, expectations, salary levels and market trends relating to their specialist area. Clients leverage this niche knowledge to help plan staffing and shape job descriptions, salary levels, role functions and working conditions. Recruitment agencies also have specialist expertise when it comes to work health and safety (WHS) for on-hire employees and can provide detailed award interpretation and employment support.

Access to broader networks

When an employer is looking to hire, they will seek out the right person for the job. This means someone who can complete the duties of the position well and who aligns with the organisation's values and environment. When searching for suitable candidates, employers and recruiters may engage with both active and passive candidates. Active candidates are likely to apply via mainstream job boards and be very proactive with their job search. Passive candidates may be open to job opportunities but are unlikely to be applying for jobs regularly. Recruitment agencies can provide organisations with broader networks and better access to both active and passive candidates. They are likely to invest in subscriptions with all major job boards, back-end CV and resume databases, and many different sourcing tools and technology. They engage with niche candidates over time and build relationships and credibility in their specialist markets by providing advice, support and knowledge. This means that when an employer is seeking the right candidate, a professional recruitment consultant may already have candidates in their network, or existing relationships with candidates who they can recommend.

Strong partnerships

When job seekers engage with a professional recruitment consultant, they can build up a high level of rapport and trust over time. This means that your consultant can bring you the right job opportunities based on your career goals. Similarly, as a recruitment consultant partners with an organisation, they get to know them over time and understand their environment, goals and work ethic. They can understand which candidates may align with their culture and values. As an advocate of both the candidate and the organisation, the recruitment consultant can strengthen both of their reputations in the market and communicate their EVPs effectively.

Time and cost savings

Organisations that partner with a professional recruitment agency can benefit from significant time and cost savings. Outsourcing the recruitment process can allow organisations to stay focussed on their core duties and areas of expertise. According to the Society for Human Resource Management (SHRM), the average time it takes to fill a position is 36 days. If you're an employer recruiting directly, that's 36 days of writing advertisements, answering questions, screening CVs, phone-screening applicants, interviewing and shortlisting. And that's all before conducting any proactive passive candidate sourcing. This can incur huge costs for employers, so they may choose to outsource their recruitment to a professional recruitment agency.

How recruitment agencies can assist you

Whether you're looking to access jobs that aren't available on mainstream job boards or need some career support and advice, a recruitment agency can support your job search positively and help fast-track you into interviews and jobs. Just like if you are training for a big sport event, it helps to have a coach. Recruitment consultants are incredibly knowledgeable about their specialist markets and have a wealth of information and insights. You can leverage this knowledge, build great relationships and be introduced to clients who have a high level of trust in their recruitment partners. It helps to have someone in your corner who can manage client expectations and ensure that you are presented only with fair, market-competitive and appropriate job offers.

Recruitment consultants can really understand your key drivers, motivations and what you want in your life, based on what you tell them. They can advocate for flexibility in your employment and help you gain a better level of work-life balance. If you are open with your consultant about your true motivations, they can help you to find the right match and maintain confidentiality along the way. Whether it's working close to home, finding a great mentor to learn from in your job or earning more money, a recruitment consultant can match jobs to your true priorities and advocate for your preferences. A quality recruitment agency will not just assess you against jobs that they have, but they can work strategically with you on your career as a trusted adviser. Your preferences may change over time – the employment you want while, for example, studying at university may differ from what you'd seek after graduation, or after having a family. A good recruitment agency can partner with you at any life stage.

Recruitment agencies can also promote diversity and inclusion. They are well trained in antidiscrimination and will actively promote broader thinking and perspectives. I can think of many times when a client has come into a job-brief session with a narrow view of 'culture fit'. Recruiters are often provided with defined criteria that can make the job inaccessible to candidates who could otherwise do the job very well. They can work actively to broaden this view and the criteria against which they are recruiting to make the brief more inclusive and accessible to diverse populations. Even if a candidate doesn't meet the strict criteria of the employer, recruitment agencies may choose to advocate for the candidate and demonstrate how they can successfully work in the position. This is often relevant to ensure balanced shortlists and open the client's mind to potential candidates that they may have otherwise overlooked. The employer may not even realise that the criteria they have set for the recruitment process is biased towards particular candidates. By gently, or sometimes overtly, influencing attitudes and approaches to recruitment, agencies have helped promote diversity and inclusion in many workplaces.

Recruitment agencies can help place you into temporary, contract or permanent work, and support you as an employee during on-hire assignments. Recruiters are experts in identifying transferable skills too. They may highlight skills to an employer that you can bring across from other jobs or industries and put you forward for positions that you may otherwise have been overlooked for. You can even gain work through an agency in different locations, and your reputation and work preferences can be shared across different branches, where permission is given by you.

Case study

Darryl is an air-conditioner mechanic and initially worked in Darwin, then overseas in England for five years. After returning to Australia, he registered with a recruitment agency who offered him positions in both Darwin and rural New South Wales (NSW). Loving the country, he chose the regional location and worked there for a couple of years. His partner was then offered work in Adelaide and they decided to make the move. Because Darryl has a great reputation and relationship with the recruitment agency who placed him in NSW, they were able to immediately offer him work from their Adelaide branch without him having to re-register or even interview with the client. Darryl enjoys the strong relationship that he has with the recruitment agency who looks after his employment and provides great support and advice.

While recruitment consultants are paid by the employer that is offering the position available, they can still offer valuable career advice and support to candidates. Several initiatives have been set up to make recruitment consultants available to even more job seekers.

> **Case study**
>
> In 2018, RCSA launched 'Meet a Recruiter', a program designed to support job seekers looking for advice and guidance on how to overcome obstacles in their job search. Consultants from a host of different recruitment agencies across Australia and New Zealand came together to meet one on one with candidates. They offered free advice, support and knowledge from years of experience. Candidates were able to access advice on CV and resume writing, interview preparation, online branding and effective job-search techniques. The initiative was rolled out nationally and continues today.

Loveyourworkanz.org and Workingsooner.com asked Australian agency workers in 2020 why they love working the way that they do. Here are just some of the reasons they gave:

- 'Agency work lets me choose when and where I work. I'm in control.'
- 'Agency work pays me for every hour I work.'
- 'Agency work is diverse and varied.'
- 'Agency work allows me to travel.'
- 'Agency work allows me to work in different workplaces.'

- 'Agency work presents new and different opportunities.'
- 'Agency work allows me to try out different jobs before committing to one.'
- 'Agency work keeps me connected to the workforce as a mature worker.'
- 'Agency work allows me to balance work with life.'
- 'Agency work allows me to care for my kids and work when I am available.'
- 'Agency work helped me transition careers.'
- 'Agency work allows me to be certain I am getting paid my legal entitlements.'
- 'Agency work gives me freedom.'

How to identify a professional recruitment agency

A professional recruitment agency will have a number of key characteristics which you can research and look out for before making contact. From flexible work arrangements to diverse career opportunities, there are many ways that recruitment agencies can enhance your employment and support your life and career goals. Following are the top seven questions to ask yourself to ensure that you are partnering with a quality recruitment agency.

1. Do they hold professional membership?

Professional membership of the World Employment Confederation (WEC) and its associated international members can give you confidence that a recruitment agency is committed to high standards and professional ethics, and keeps up to date with market trends, regulations and requirements. In Australia, choose a recruitment agency who is a member of The Recruitment, Consulting & Staffing Association (RCSA) to be sure that you are engaging with a professional agency; they have a member directory available to search at rcsa.com.au. Member agencies are required to keep their skills and knowledge up to date through regular professional development and industry briefings. They must also adhere to a binding code of conduct for professional practice. If you ever have any issues in your dealings with a recruitment agency, and they are a member of RCSA, then you can also contact RCSA for support. This gives you an added layer of insurance and confidence. For other countries you can view the WEC list of members at wecglobal.org to select an agency that is committed to high professional standards.

2. Are they a licensed provider?

In many countries, including Australia, certain states require companies to hold a labour hire licence to engage on-hire employees. Licences can also be required to engage permanent employees, and perform recruitment or employment services. The intention of this government regulation is to protect workers' rights and eliminate rogue behaviour. If you are a casual employee looking for temporary, contract or permanent employment, be sure to engage with a licensed recruitment agency in regions where a licence is legally required. Working with a licensed provider helps to ensure that you are engaging with an agency that is meeting their legal obligations, and gives you greater protection and support in regard to your workplace rights, WHS, pay and entitlements. Accreditation and assurance programs such as StaffSure offer an added layer of confidence in relation to compliance, and can help you ensure that the owners operating particular recruitment and staffing agencies are fit to do so. Check your local government authority website, such as labourhireauthority.vic.gov.au, to discover requirements for your location and view a list of licenced recruitment agencies.

3. Do they work on retained and exclusive assignments?

When discussing a position with a recruitment agency, it's fair to ask whether the position is exclusive to their company. A good recruitment agency will work on mostly retained and exclusive assignments. This means that the employer has only briefed one recruitment agency on the position and that they are entrusted with the end-to-end process. For you as a candidate, this reduces confusion and speaks highly of the agency's partnership status with the organisation that they are representing. Retained assignments are where the recruitment agency has been paid an engagement fee upfront to recruit the position. Exclusive and retained work indicates a recruitment agency that is highly regarded and trusted by their clients. They will have built this reputation over time and are much more likely to treat your career and job search with the care, attention and professionalism that it deserves.

4. Are they knowledgeable, supportive and thorough?

A good recruitment agency will have consultants who are well trained and knowledgeable, and act as professional advisers. They can give you advice on your career, CV, job search and the interview process, and work hard to negotiate quality work conditions, contracts, salaries and benefits. They will give you an indication of what employers are offering, jobs that are available and which positions could be a good fit for you. Recruitment consultants who have a high level of trust from their clients will often be able to arrange an interview for you or place you immediately into jobs that may not be publicly available. This is due to their strong relationships with their clients – who trust their opinion and recommendations – and access to unlisted vacancies. Recruitment agencies can also help you access jobs that may expand your career goals and thinking.

> **Case study**
>
> Aaron was a graduate civil engineer who was in his final year at university. During this time, he took on agency work in construction to supplement his income. He enjoyed the flexibility, with days and hours which fit around his study. While originally Aaron thought that he wanted to be involved in design, he discovered through agency work that he actually loved construction and was interested in pursuing construction project management. He was working as a labourer on a site in Queensland when the site foreman found

out in casual conversation that he was studying civil engineering. He was recommended by the foreman to the project manager and offered a graduate civil engineering opportunity on a path to project management. Aaron attributes his 'foot in the door' to agency work, giving him an edge with hands-on experience working on industrial and residential estates. He felt that this experience put him ahead of other candidates and fast-tracked his path to permanent employment in his chosen field, in line with his career goals.

When briefing you on positions, recruitment consultants will have an excellent level of knowledge of the organisation that they are representing and the job that they are recruiting for. They will be thorough in their approach and forthcoming with information once you have been shortlisted. Part of their job is to help you prepare effectively for your interview with the employer or host, or for your first day on the job. They will ensure that you have all of the information that you need. By having a detailed understanding of the job and company, you can make an informed decision about whether you are interested in progressing further. There are plenty of quality recruitment agencies out there that would love to work with you, so make sure that you select a knowledgeable, supportive and thorough recruitment partner to entrust your career to.

5. Do they represent quality organisations?

Established, professional recruitment agencies are selective about which organisations they choose to represent. They won't just work for anybody and aren't prepared to recommend poor jobs or work environments to their candidates. A good recruitment agency will represent organisations who display a positive work environment, fair pay and conditions, and are progressive and innovative in their approach. They gather feedback through their own market research and from talking to hundreds of candidates each month. They often have inside knowledge of which organisations are a pleasure to work with and which are not. They will work hard to engage with the best employers in the market, and in turn can connect you with them too.

6. Are they specialist consultants?

When choosing a recruitment agency, try to build partnerships with consultants who specialise specifically in your profession or industry. They will have deep vertical knowledge of your area of expertise and will have built credibility with employers in that space. They can provide advice on salaries, benefits, work environments, market trends and your career. By proactively reaching out and ensuring that your details are registered with them, they can keep you front-of-mind for upcoming positions.

If your skills and experience are extremely niche and are in demand by employers, a specialist recruitment agency can even build a list of clients that they would like to speak to about your background and preferences. This can uncover job opportunities that may not have been advertised. In many situations, employers may not be advertising a job, but they may have briefed their recruitment partner to look out for candidates with certain types of experience. They ask the agency to contact them once suitable candidates have been interviewed and assessed. This allows employers to be alerted when quality niche candidates become available on the market and are interested in job opportunities.

7. Do they display excellent communication?

You'll receive regular updates from your recruitment agency with job opportunities, career advice and support for your job search. These might be in the form of phone calls, emails, company blogs, job alerts, dedicated interview preparation information and social media communications. If you've applied for a job, you should receive an email or phone-based update within two weeks in regard to your progress. If you haven't received this, it's a great idea to give your recruitment agency a call to check in. If interviewed, you should receive prompt phone-based interview feedback and advice on next steps. You should always be informed of where your CV is going and give permission to the agency to represent you to each organisation. A good recruiter will keep you informed throughout the recruitment process as you progress through each interview and assessment stage. They can gather detailed feedback from clients and support you with advice regarding interview preparation and key company information. Most importantly, they should return your calls and emails promptly and professionally. A good recruitment agency can also provide you with a variety of job opportunities and help facilitate a smooth job-search process through detailed, honest and clear information.

> **Case study**
>
> Louise is a nurse who loves to travel for work. She completed her first job out of university with a recruitment agency on a remote island off the east coast of Australia. She felt that she had better peace of mind knowing that the recruitment agency had assessed the employer first, inspected the worksite and could even describe to her what the environment was like. The agency provided a third-party opinion of the employer that was objective, transparent and honest. They talked about the benefits of working there but also the challenges. It allowed Louise to really assess the pros and cons of working on the island before uprooting her life and moving halfway across the country. Thanks to the agency providing a high level of information and detail about the position prior to her accepting the job, Louise was very satisfied with her work environment and duties, and thoroughly enjoyed the employer's culture and working style. It was a great match. Over a long career, Louise has gone on to complete many assignments through the same recruitment agency, which knows her well, understands her preferences and finds her work that fits within her career goals.

What to expect when you register with a recruitment agency

An invitation to interview with a recruitment agency is usually offered once you are identified as a good fit for a current position. Agencies are hired by employers to help them find talented individuals for particular positions. This means that they won't be able to interview every candidate that approaches them. Having a phone conversation is still valuable, though, as the recruiter may be able to talk to you about current positions, give you an indication of the frequency and type of roles that come up, and provide some career advice and support. They can clarify which positions you are targeting and can keep you front-of-mind. In some cases, an agency might invite you to interview and register ahead of job vacancies. This is usually offered to candidates with niche skills which are currently in demand by employers. In this situation you can choose to attend the interview or wait until a job arises. Registering in advance can be an advantage, as this can avoid delays in the recruitment process and give you access to more jobs.

If you are invited to an interview with a recruitment agency, you can expect to receive a confirmation email with details and next steps. They may request documents to verify identity and visa status and validate education listed on your CV. During your interview, your consultant will brief you directly on job opportunities available, particularly in regard to the specific jobs that you have applied for. They will give you honest, on-the-spot feedback about where you sit in regard to the client's criteria and candidate preferences for the job. If you meet the level of experience, skills and requirements that the client has, they may offer to arrange an interview for you with the hiring organisation. You will be given ample opportunity to ask questions about the employer and the job, and for advice on interview preparation. You may also be asked to complete a range of assessments prior to, during or after the interview. We will cover these in more detail in Chapter 11. Allow an hour for the interview, or longer if assessments will be completed onsite. You can always check with your consultant how long you should allocate on the day.

Your recruitment consultant is there to support your job search and provide advice. Remember that they speak with hundreds of candidates each month, so being proactive and providing them with email or phone updates about changes in your job search or career can be helpful. To stay in touch with your recruitment consultant regarding job opportunities, connect with them via email and on LinkedIn. You can also follow them on Twitter, Instagram and other professional social media pages. Sign up for job alerts on the agency's website, if these are available, to be notified of positions when they match your job-search criteria.

Once you are registered with them, a good recruitment agency will keep in touch with you regularly to see if you might be a match for any current job opportunities. They will update your file each time you speak with them, to reflect your preferences and whether you have secured work or not. If you are successful in progressing through to the interview stage for a position, your recruitment consultant will provide you with support and advice throughout the recruitment process. They can negotiate work conditions, salary and benefits with the employer on your behalf and ensure that you are kept up to date. They will typically manage all communication – outside of formal client interviews – until an offer is made and accepted. They can even help set up your induction and will stay in touch for months after you have started to ensure that you are happy and settling in well.

If you are registered for temp, contract and on-hire opportunities, you may be offered jobs without requiring an interview with the host company. If you are interested in progressing, the recruitment agency will brief you fully, get you set up for your first day and provide WHS support. There is often a tight deadline for the agency to fill the job, so you'll need to let them know quickly whether you are interested. The agency will often act as your employer throughout and provide you with pay and payroll support. You can talk to them about your experiences onsite, keep them updated on how you are enjoying the position and ask for help when needed. When offered a temp or contract opportunity, it's important to show loyalty and commitment, and communicate frequently. If you're not enjoying the job you have commenced, let your recruitment agency know and they can help to improve conditions with your employer or discuss alternative employment options.

It's best to register with one or two recruitment agencies initially and give them an opportunity to present jobs to you. If you register with too many agencies, it can be difficult for you to manage communication and keep track of where you are being represented. If you make it clear to the recruitment agency that you are only happy to be put forward for positions that you have discussed together, then you can avoid confusion about which agency has represented you to the job.

Respecting the relationships that recruitment agencies have with their clients is key. Sometimes these relationships can span decades. This is just one of many reasons why recruitment agencies can help you get an edge during your job search and throughout your career.

> ### ☕ Coffee break
>
> Recruitment agencies can support your career in many ways. Select an agency that is a member of a professional industry association such as the WEC or RCSA, and ensure that the agency is a licensed provider in states where this is legally required. Mostly retained or exclusive work can indicate a high level of trust between the agency and the organisations that choose to partner with them. This can reflect an agency that will treat your career with great care, respect and consideration. A professional recruitment consultant will be knowledgeable, supportive and thorough in their approach. They will represent quality organisations, specialise deeply in particular markets and provide excellent communication and information.
>
> Now that you have started your job search, applied for positions and built a great relationship with a quality recruitment agency, it's time to look at screening and assessment processes and prepare for your interview.

Chapter 11

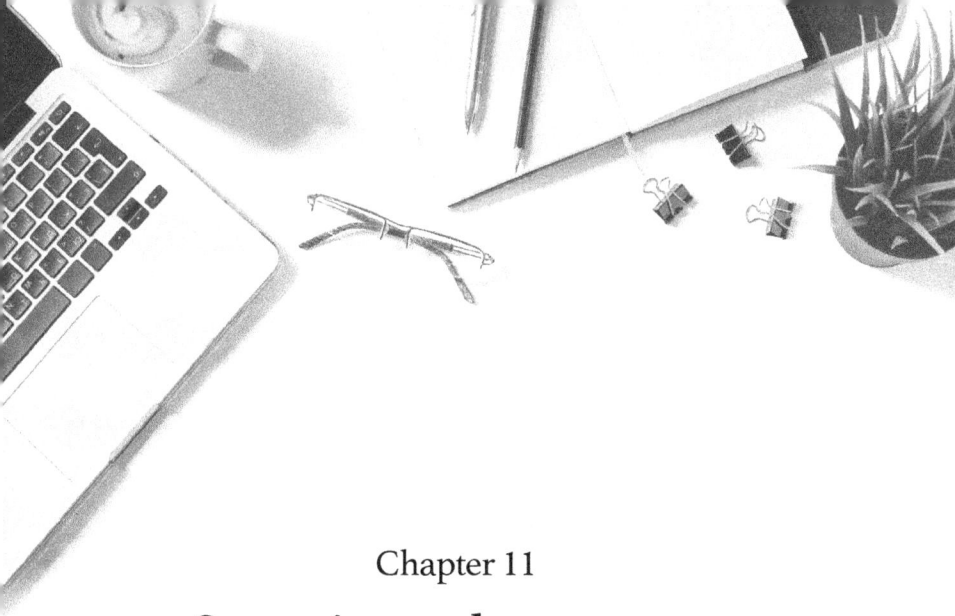

Screening and assessment

- Understand screening, assessment and credentialling processes.
- Excel during phone screens and video interviewing.
- Prepare for IQ, skills and task-based tests, assessment centres and behavioural profiling.
- Explore chat bots, gamification, job simulation and functional assessments.

Case study

Rami's heart is pounding. He's nearly at level ten. Each time he's competed a level he seems to have gotten faster and faster, but this one is tricky. He'll have to work together with other players to decide on the number and configuration of blocks that they need to build the bridge across the river. He wants to take the lead and do it all himself, but he knows it has to be a team effort. 'What do you think?' he asks player number four. 'Three across and 18 along I think is the right answer. How about you?' This goes back and forth for a while until finally all of the players are across the river safely. The game is finished, over, complete. Somehow Rami feels that it's not who gets to the other side first that matters but how they got there as a team.

And he's right. It's the call he gets later from the internal recruitment manager that confirms his hunch is true. 'We loved your approach to teamwork, Rami', she says, impressed also with his problem-solving skills and quick thinking. 'We'd love you to join the team.'

There are many different approaches to screening and assessment throughout the recruitment process. Whether it's gamification, questionnaires or chat bots, the end goal is the same – to assess your skills, capabilities and fit for the job. Let's explore the different types of screening and assessments and how you can excel in completing them.

Phone screening

Once you have submitted your application for a job, you may receive a phone call to discuss your application further. This is known as a 'phone screen' and provides the employer or recruitment agency with valuable information about your career goals, job preferences, skills and experience. It's a great opportunity for you to communicate why you are an excellent candidate for the job and how you could add value if appointed. You may be asked about your:

- interest in the position
- current job
- previous positions – and which of them you have enjoyed and why
- current and desired salary
- location and travel preferences
- experience, skills and education
- experience with different systems
- experience in different industries
- career goals
- availability and work preferences.

To make a great impression during a phone screen, ensure that you can talk freely and be friendly, professional and forthcoming. Keep your answers short and to the point; allow the employer or recruiter to ask further information as needed. Prepare in advance for the topics listed above and keep this information to hand, such as on your phone, in case you are out and about when called. Keep your Employee Value Proposition front-of-mind to ensure that you sell yourself well. You can also ask some questions about the position. If you're invited in for an interview, be sure to clarify what you need to prepare, how long to allocate and location details. Thank the employer for calling you, and convey that you look forward to hearing about next steps.

Questionnaires

You may be asked to fill out a questionnaire during the application process or prior to interview. Questions asked may be similar to those for phone screening. They are typically used to identify candidates who meet the minimum criteria. For example, if you're applying for a physiotherapy position in Australia, you must be registered with the Physiotherapy Board of Australia. Employers may have a questionnaire attached to the job application that asks questions such as, 'Are you registered with the Physiotherapy Board of Australia?' or, 'Do you hold permanent residency in Australia or a visa with working rights?' It's best to answer these questions honestly, clearly and concisely. Sometimes questionnaires are simply in place to gather registration details prior to an interview and do not form part of the assessment process.

Chat bots and AI

You may encounter chat bots during your application process, which are a form of artificial intelligence. Chat bots can ask questions, learn about your preferences and provide education about the recruitment process and what to expect next. They can simulate a real conversation, providing tailored questions and answers depending on your previous responses. If you say yes to a question, you may be taken in one direction, whereas if you say no, you may be taken in another direction. For example, if you are registering with a recruitment agency for temporary employment and indicate 'yes' to this preference, the chat bot might start to ask you questions related to temporary employment and walk you through the applicable registration process. If you say that you're interested in permanent positions, then the chat bot would screen you for permanent opportunities only and direct you towards questions and information relating to permanent employment.

> **Case study**
>
> people2people has a chat bot called 'Pete'. When candidates are successful through the initial phone-screening process with a recruitment consultant, they are sent a confirmation email for their interview. Included is a link to click on to speak with Pete. He asks candidates questions about their work preferences, registration details and salary range, as well as where they would like to work and how far they are happy to travel. Pete can even ask more role-specific questions and prepare candidates for their interview. This experience replaces the old-school clipboard and paper that used to be handed out to candidates in the agency waiting room. Instead, they are able to complete their details in advance on their computer, tablet or phone, and do it at their convenience. If they still prefer paper then this is available too, but Pete certainly provides a convenient alternative that is efficient, intelligent, personalised and better for the environment.

Expect to see more AI automation, chat bots and personalisation in the future throughout recruitment processes.

ID and visa checks

When an employer or recruiter meets with you, it's important that they can verify that you are who you say you are. In many cases this is actually legally required. You may be asked to show your passport or provide a copy. If you don't have a passport, then often a driver's licence or birth certificate is used. Provide visa details where applicable so that the recruiter can check your visa status with the immigration department in your country. Just taking your word for it unfortunately won't be enough, as severe penalties apply in most countries for employing workers illegally. ID and visa checks are built into every quality recruitment process, so it's a great idea to have the documents to hand and even bring copies to your interview. Make sure that you always keep personal identification information secure and read the employer or recruitment agency's privacy policy in advance.

Skills testing

Skills testing can include software assessments – such as for Microsoft Office, Adobe Photoshop, CAD or Xero – and are intended to ascertain your level of knowledge in finding your way around the program. They can also assess your ability to complete certain tasks. Getting 100% is not always the goal, as some jobs only require a basic or intermediate level of competency. In contrast, if you're a financial accountant or data analyst undertaking a software assessment for a program that you have used previously, the expectation may be that you are competent to an advanced level. Make sure that you advise your recruiter which version of the software program you have used in the past, as testing you on a different version of the software program is stressful for you and useless for them.

Assessments may be given for individual skills too, such as typing, maths, vocabulary and verbal or numerical reasoning. Some testing focuses on broader skill sets within a profession, such as customer service, sales, accounts receivable, front desk procedures, hospitality or retail merchandising. You'll be asked a series of questions relating to the key area to understand your level of skill.

Skills testing is often undertaken onsite at the employer or recruiter's office, or is sometimes sent to you to be completed online. If maths is involved, be sure to clarify whether a calculator can be used, as this is the case in many testing scenarios. Ensure that you are free from distraction and focus on both speed and quality. It's a great idea to do some practice assessments online beforehand; there are plenty of free versions publicly available. Tests are often timed and reviewed to assess efficiency. There are also some tests which have a time limit. Try to complete all questions before the time limit, but remember that many people don't and that it won't be the deciding factor for whether you get the job or not. It's just one piece of the puzzle.

Behavioural profiling

American psychologist Paul E. Meehl explored in detail the concept that past behaviour predicts future behaviour. After years of empirical research, he was able to predict human behaviour in many different scenarios. Employers often undertake behavioural profiling to try to understand how employees might act in different situations once employed. They may build a job profile and define a preferred range of results that they would like to see for particular characteristics such as energy, attitude, flexibility and objective thinking. The range will be different for each characteristic and may change depending on the job. Some organisations assess their highest performing employees and build a hiring profile based on the average of their results. They will then look to hire people whose results fall close to the average of their highest performing people.

Employers look for different characteristics based on the position. Leadership positions often require a high level of communication skill, decisiveness and optimism, while graduate positions may require lower levels of independence and higher levels of manageability. A salesperson may be expected to have high levels of energy, sociability and empathy, while an accounts payable clerk will require a high level of accuracy and detail.

When completing a behavioural profiling test, expect to be asked similar questions multiple times. By doing this, the assessment checks whether your behaviour might change depending on the context. If you answer the same way every time, your result will likely fall at one of the far ends of the scale. If your answers are mixed, then you are likely to have a more neutral result that's closer to the average. It is difficult to know whether the employer is looking for a low, high or average response to a question, so it's best not to overthink it. Instead, if you are asked to complete a behavioural profiling assessment, ensure that you have allocated at least an hour to undertake the test, are free from distraction and answer based on your first instinct. Completing some practice assessments first can help solidify your thoughts too. If you answer each question honestly and based on your first instinct, you will have a more accurate profile. This means that if you are hired, you're likely to be matched with an employer that has aligned values, provides you with autonomy and allows you to thrive using your natural working style.

Ensuring a good behavioural match is key to you enjoying your job. If your preference is to use your right hand for writing and you're asked to use your left, you're likely to be able to give it a go, but it won't be very comfortable. The same goes for your employment – working in a job that is a poor match to your natural personality can be draining and demotivating. While it used to be a widely held belief that your personality is set in stone throughout adulthood, more recent research found that certain personality traits tend to become weaker or stronger over time. These changes manifest slowly though, not overnight. Set yourself up for enjoyment and success by finding an employer and job that appreciates your natural abilities and personality traits. It could lead to a long and fulfilling career.

Intelligence testing

Using a standard test to assess human intelligence, employers can receive a total score called an 'intelligence quotient' (IQ). It's less commonly used by employers today and is often replaced with behavioural profiling. If you are required to complete an IQ test, you can expect questions about mathematics, spatial awareness, relationships between objects, verbal reasoning, language ability, memory and problem solving. It's a great idea to do some practice assessments in advance to get yourself prepared.

Video interviewing

Before being invited in for a face-to-face interview, you may be interviewed by the organisation's video interviewing platform. Companies like Spark Hire, myInterview, HireVue, Sonru and Vieple offer software that helps to facilitate the interview process for employers. The benefits for employers include reduced time in filling jobs and cost savings, while candidates gain the opportunity to showcase their capabilities, skills and experience. Video interviewing provides organisations with particular insights into the candidate's communication skills and allows candidates to tailor their response to the job. Sometimes the interview simulates real life, where the candidate is asked the question and needs to answer in real time. In other scenarios, candidates can record and re-record their answers multiple times until they are happy with the version they would like to submit. AI is also used to assess facial expressions, words and answers, and shortlist candidates based on their match to the job. This technology is in its infancy but is already used by major organisations in Australia, the US and the UK for call centre and frontline positions. Companies that deliver this software have built in protections for unlawful discrimination in each country. Refer to Chapter 8 for how to present professionally on video.

Gamification

Fancy playing a video game as part of your interview process? With gamification, employers can turn often dull tests and assessments into interactive experiences. Gamification is where the mechanics of games are brought into non-game environments to make them more interesting. A great example might be testing sales candidates via a treasure hunt game, during which they have to solve problems, take risks and digest verbal information to make decisions and find the treasure. Via a gamification method like this, employers can promote a healthy level of competition and test sales candidates' motivation and performance levels. Other games can assess for teamwork, problem solving and specific job competencies and skills. If you are asked to participate in game-based assessments, ensure that you are clear on the rules and objectives. Gamification can also give candidates an insight into the company's culture and reflect positively on their approach to recruitment. Providing candidates with a more interesting, engaging and fun recruitment process allows the organisation to stand out and be noticed.

Job simulation

An employer may want to paint a picture of what the job is like, and also assess your skills and abilities when it comes to performing the core duties of the position. They can do this via a job simulation assessment. This can be completed in person or online. In a job simulation, you will be asked to undertake activities that you'd be expected to perform if hired for the job. For example, a candidate for a barista position might be asked to prepare a coffee, while a pilot may be asked to land an imaginary plane. A copywriter may be given a press release to write; an accountant, financial statements to prepare.

Case study

When hiring prospective graduate recruitment consultants at people2people, we have often asked candidates to present our latest research report back to us or conduct a mini job-brief session. This allows us to assess communication skills, confidence, ability to think and respond quickly, interpersonal skills, data interpretation and presentation skills. Even though it is a very short 15-minute assessment, we can gain valuable information regarding possible employees. It also allows candidates to experience some of the job tasks and what it might be like to work in the role.

Task-based assessments

You may be given a short task to undertake in preparation for your interview, such as preparing a three-month sales strategy or critiquing a football game. The task will depend on the duties of the job and the skills that the employer is assessing for. A search engine optimisation specialist might have to research and recommend the top five keywords the employer should target, while a UX designer may assess customer experience through the employer's website and make three recommendations for improvement. Task-based assessments are similar to some job simulation assessments but focus on just one aspect. If asked to complete one, ensure that you are clear on the instructions and outcomes required and ask questions to clarify as needed. It's better to be sure about what you need to do upfront so you can proceed with confidence.

Assessment centres

As part of the recruitment process for a graduate program or a frontline role such as in sales, hospitality or customer service, you may be invited to an assessment centre. This is typically a multifaceted group assessment that may be attended by anywhere from five to fifty other people. Employers may set group exercises where you problem-solve together, simulate a work situation or participate in a role-play. You may be asked to verbally present to the group or undertake behavioural profiling, or verbal, numerical or reasoning tests. There may also be a presentation by the employer about what is on offer. Employers will watch for skills in problem-solving, teamwork, leadership, listening, influencing others, proactivity and communication. They will also observe whether you have a positive attitude and an inclusive approach, and how well you work with others to achieve objectives.

Prepare well, relax and be confident. Put yourself forward, but also allow others to do the same. Most of all, be positive. If you really want to stand out, come armed with some great questions for the recruiter that you can ask during breaks. Actively build one-on-one rapport with them while being respectful of their time.

Credentialling

When you tell an employer that you have a degree in computer science, and it's relevant to your job application, they will want to verify this information independently. You can make this process easier by providing certificates of qualifications, certifications and licences with your job application. If you have misplaced your original documents, most educational institutions and issuing bodies will be able to provide you with a replacement. You can simply call or email to request this. Some will charge a small administration fee, while others will provide it at no cost. It's a great idea to have these available in advance of applying for jobs to avoid any delays in the recruitment process.

Credentialling is legally required for many professions, including medicine and law. Organisations in these sectors and others are required to comply with government policies and legislation to ensure that you are fit to perform the job that you are applying for.

Police checks

Employers in some sectors require national and sometimes international police checks; such sectors include banking and financial institutions, law firms, prisons, gaming venues, and positions where employees may interact with children or vulnerable people. For some job applications it can be a distinct advantage to have your police check completed already. Employers may have an immediate temporary or permanent opportunity available, or have a tight recruitment deadline. If you can provide your valid police check certificate upfront, this can reduce delays in the recruitment process.

Working with Children Check

Providing a safe and secure environment for children is key for many employers. Such environments include schools, hospitals, sporting clubs, recreation facilities, dance schools, childcare centres and disability services. If you are applying for positions within these sectors, or for any positions that might require you to interact with children, then it's a great idea to have your Working with Children Check (WWCC) completed upfront. Submitting this along with your job application can avoid delays in the recruitment process.

Medical assessments

Good physical health and capability are essential requirements for some jobs. In these situations, you may be asked to undertake a medical assessment as part of the recruitment process. This will be completed by a medical doctor and either organised by you or by the company who may employ you. It's often requested much later in the recruitment process, after all interviews and assessments have been completed.

Functional assessment

If you are required to perform physical tasks as part of your job, you may be asked to undertake a functional assessment. This can measure your cardiovascular fitness, physical strength and whether you can complete specific tasks within the job. For example, police officers are required to be physically active within their job, and so are professional cricketers. Assessments are typically performed by occupational therapists, physiotherapists or accredited exercise physiologists. Some functional assessments are quite unconventional but can be important in assessing a person's ability to do the job safely and effectively.

> **Reflection**
>
> When I went through the recruitment process for Emirates airlines cabin crew many years ago, I remember that the very first test was a functional assessment. After the recruitment team had introduced themselves to the hundreds of waiting hopefuls, we were ushered towards a piece of paper stuck up high on the wall. This was to simulate the positioning of the hat racks which hold passenger luggage and safety equipment. It showed the height needed to comfortably reach the safety equipment in the event of an emergency on board – a pretty important part of the job! I remembered noting the height requirements for some of the Australian airlines as being not less than 163cm. Being 161cm tall, I wasn't even eligible to apply to those airlines, so you can imagine how nervous I was as I approached the piece of paper. Fortunately, years of ballet training had somehow come in handy. I got up on my tippy toes and stretched up my right arm. To my delight, I made contact with something paper-like. That little white rectangle was my first step towards a ticket around the world.

Most employers use test results as only part of the picture when assessing candidates and rarely make final decisions based on results alone. You can request a copy of your results, and sometimes the employer or recruiter can provide a post-assessment debrief. Even if you don't excel in one of the assessments, your other skills and experience may compensate for the gap.

> **Reflection**
>
> After several months travelling the world with Emirates, I remember meeting a crew member on board who was a little bit shorter than me. I was curious as to how she might have passed the functional assessment required. In chatting with her later, she mentioned

casually that she spoke seven languages. Seven! 'Okay', I thought, 'I'll shut the hat racks and you can speak to the passengers'. Clearly her language skills were incredibly impressive, and Emirates wasn't going to pass them up, or her great personality, because of one little assessment.

Auditions

You may have seen the audition scene from the movie *La La Land* or been required to audition for a school play once upon a time. Auditions are a real part of the recruitment process for actors, singers, dancers, circus performers, poets, musicians, comedians and other artists. An audition is a way for candidates to demonstrate their practical abilities and skills. For example, an actor might deliver the lines and performance of a scene from a movie, and a dancer may complete a group class or solo observed by the employer.

> **Reflection**
>
> As a former dancer auditioning for opportunities, I can understand the nerves that many candidates experience during auditions and interviews. After an audition, I would often be standing there among 200 other dancers, hands shaking and heart pounding. We would each be wearing an identifying number and waiting to hear if ours was called out, indicating that we had made it through to the next round. The wait could feel endless, and the outcome sometimes crushing, but every now and then, luck would come to the surface.

Auditions are possibly the most nerve-racking experience for an artist but can certainly lead to landing some of the best jobs worldwide. Auditions can be completed live or recorded and submitted along with your job application. Some professions require a 'showreel' or a video of a recent performance.

☕ Coffee break

As part of each recruitment process, you may be exposed to lots of different screening and assessment techniques, including phone screens, questionnaires, video interviewing, speaking with chat bots and undertaking ID and visa checks. You might complete behavioural profiling or an IQ test, or skills or task-based assessments. The employer might make it a little more fun with gamification or job simulation. Be prepared for credentialling and any requests for a Police Check or Working with Children Check by having your certificates ready to go. If you have to complete a medical or functional assessment, being in good physical condition can help. For an audition, you can prepare a piece that you are comfortable with, get there early, take some deep breaths and remember how amazing you are.

Throughout each stage of the recruitment process, a friendly, positive approach and great rapport-building will get you very far. Keep your Employee Value Proposition in mind and be confident about the value that you can add to the right employer. Whether you're 30 years into your career or fresh out of university, you've got a lot of skills and experience that you can bring to the table. By articulating your strengths and drawing attention to relevant experience, you can really make an employer notice you. If you've been invited to an interview, you are one step closer to getting the job that you *really* want.

Now, let's prepare ahead of your interview and set you up for success.

Part V
Interview for success

Chapter 12

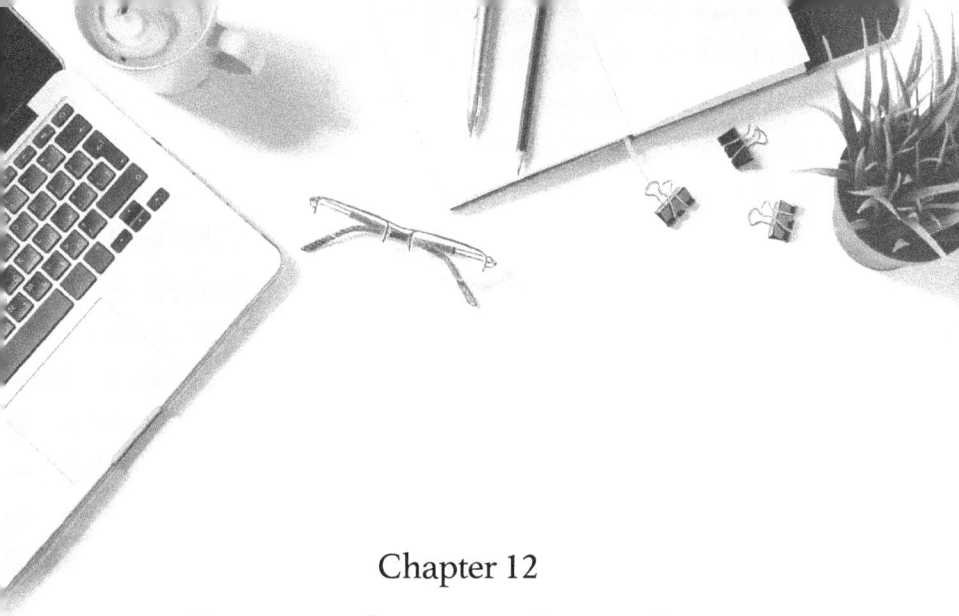

Prepare for your interview

- Conduct detailed research on the company, job and interviewers.
- Prepare responses to common and behavioural-based interview questions.
- Complete paperwork and assessments, and make plans for your interview day.

You've got the call you were hoping for: the interview is booked for next week. It's taken weeks of applications and phone screens, and at times it was pretty tough, but you've finally got there. You know that only a small portion of candidates are invited in for interview, so you're feeling pretty happy right now. You know that the hard work doesn't stop here, though, and that there is plenty of preparation ahead. You set aside some time, get your thinking cap on and get ready to put pen to paper. It's time to ensure that you stand out during your interview and have the best chance of landing that job.

What can you do to make yourself stand out during an interview and really be noticed? How can you get the edge? After many years interviewing thousands of candidates for different types of positions, I can tell you that there is one thing that sets good candidates apart from others: *Preparation.*

It's the people who take the time to prepare in advance of their interview that really stand out. There are many elements to this process. Let's explore them further so that you're ready to move ahead with calmness and confidence.

Review details and complete pre-interview steps

Most recruitment agencies and internal recruitment teams will send you a confirmation email with details of your interview time, location and other requirements. They may provide a link to complete further details in advance and request information in relation to work preferences, location, visa details, identification documentation, certificates, salary information and referees.

You may also be asked to complete one of the screening or assessment processes covered in Chapter 11, such as skills testing, video interviewing or behavioural profiling. Read the instructions carefully in the confirmation email and complete all of the required documentation and assessments as early as possible. This gives your interviewer time to review what you have submitted in advance of your interview and avoids the 'I like to leave things to the last minute' vibe. If you are unclear about any part of the instructions for your interview or assessments, give your contact a call. This shows your attention to detail and desire to be clear about instructions before proceeding – a key skill required in many jobs.

Get your documents in order

Whether you're asked for them or not, it's a great idea to bring several types of documentation to your interview and be extra prepared.

First, bring three or more copies of your CV to your interview – one for you and one for each of the interviewers – and ensure that they are well tailored to the job. You may have learnt more about the job during your recent phone screen, so incorporate any updates to your CV that sell you well for the job. Having hard copies on the day gives you a distinct advantage. First, the interviewer may be busy and might not have a hard copy to hand; you can save them the hassle and embarrassment and hand one straight over. Secondly, you are leaving them with a physical reminder of you. It might even sit on their desk for a couple of days and keep your name front-of-mind. Next, tailor and prepare three hard copies of your cover letter for the position, and attach one to the back of each copy of your CV.

If you work in a visual medium or can showcase examples of your work, bring them along to the interview. A copywriter might bring some campaign examples, an architect could bring plans and a graphic designer some samples of what they have designed. Within marketing, a full portfolio is the norm, so bring this along on the day.

Next, gather your ID documents, such as your passport or birth certificate. You can save time at the interview by photocopying them now and bringing a spare copy along to provide to the interviewer. This shows your proactivity, forward-thinking approach and empathy for their time. Always be careful with how you handle identification information and keep track of originals and copies. Shred or destroy copies and originals completely when they are no longer needed. Read the organisations' privacy policy before submitting any information; this is often available publicly online via their company website.

If you hold a current visa, bring details of this along in the form of your visa confirmation letter, visa number or certificate. The recruiter or employer will need to verify your qualifications where relevant to the job and may undertake full credentialling. Save them time and effort by bringing originals and copies along of certificates, academic records and confirmation letters.

If you have prepared in advance by getting a Working with Children Check, Police Check, first-aid certificate, driver's licence, forklift licence, or any other licence or certificate that you may require, then also bring copies and originals to your interview. The interviewer may need to sight the originals in person and then retain a copy for their records, so it pays to bring both along.

Every interaction counts

You may not realise it, but your interviewer will factor in your communication style, timeliness and approach to the recruitment process outside of interviews as much as what you do and say in your interview. They will take note of whether you follow instructions well, are proactive and keep commitments such as following up with documentation, and may even look at how you treat their receptionist. Every interaction that you have with the company can form part of their opinion of you and influence your chances of landing the job. Be friendly, responsive, approachable and authentic and you won't have any worries at all.

Research, research, research

A cursory glance at the company's website isn't going to cut it in the current job market. There's a lot more information that you'll need, and taking time to review it will be worth your while. Let's look at the most important areas to research before your interview and how:

- **Company:** Look at the company's website, careers page, social media pages and, if available, annual report. Search for recent news articles about the company and read up on what might be affecting their business.
- **Job:** Read the job advertisement and position description (if provided) in more detail, and highlight keywords and criteria. You can use this to prepare responses to possible interview questions.

- **Interviewers:** Look at the profiles of your interviewers on LinkedIn and in the 'About Us' or 'Team' sections of the company website.
- **Competitors:** If you work in a niche industry and know who else might be interviewing for the position, conduct some research on their background. This helps you to understand which of your strengths to emphasise and may give you a competitive advantage.

Here are some great questions to ask and answer as best you can throughout your research:

- Who is the organisation, and what is their mission, vision and values?
- How many people are in the organisation, and where does this position fit within the organisational structure?
- What are the key requirements of the position?
- What are the key challenges of this position going to be?
- Can you identify previous candidates who have filled this position? What have they done well in the position and what could be improved?
- What are the positions and backgrounds of the people who will be interviewing you for the role?
- What are they looking for in a prospective candidate?
- What might they be concerned about when looking at your background and experience, and how can you overcome this?
- What makes you a standout candidate for the job?

Prepare responses

When a politician gets in front of a camera to do a television interview, they don't just 'wing it'. They are clear on their key messages and what to say no matter what questions are asked of them. The same goes for a dancer or an actor about to perform. They have rehearsed their choreography or lines meticulously and are ready to get out on stage. If they have prepared well, they can just relax during the performance and the moves or lines come to them naturally.

> **Reflection**
>
> As a dancer in the Australian Ballet, I used to rehearse choreography over and over again to ensure that it was second nature. I would use visualisation, and often rehearse solos two or three times in a row, knowing that if I could sustain that level of intensity in rehearsal, then when I went out on stage, it would feel much easier. This allowed me to go into each performance feeling confident and relaxed, and to enjoy the experience.
>
> The same concept can apply to interviews. If you prepare in advance and have clarity on your key messages, you can relax and be yourself on the day.

Understand your EVP for the position

In Chapter 2, we explored your Employee Value Proposition and how to develop it. There is no more important time to communicate your EVP than during your interview. Bring this firmly into focus. Put yourself in the shoes of the interviewer and think about what they will be looking for in a prospective candidate, and tailor your EVP to pitch well to this. For example, if you think that the coding skills and knowledge you have of a particular software package might be an advantage for the job, make sure that you mention it several times throughout the interview. Write down the top three to four advantages that you offer as a candidate for the role, and keep them firmly in your mind. Following are a couple of examples.

Candidate for a legal assistant position within property:
- Advanced Aderant skills – practice management software
- 75 wpm typing speed
- Three years conveyancing and property team experience
- Five years experience as a legal assistant

Candidate for a Managing Director position within fast-moving consumer goods (FMCG) manufacturing:
- Eight years executive leadership experience with full P&L responsibility
- 12 years working within FMCG
- Five years running a manufacturing facility with Lean methodology
- MBA qualified

By coming back to these key points within your responses to interview questions, you are more likely to sell yourself well for the position. Your EVP will change a little bit depending on the position and company, so think about what makes you a standout candidate for the job before you arrive at your interview.

Prepare responses to commonly asked interview questions

Here are some examples of commonly asked interview questions:
- Tell me about yourself.
- Why are you interested in this position?
- Why are you leaving your current position, or why did you leave your past position?
- Where would you like to be in five years' time, and how does this position factor into that pathway?
- What are the three greatest achievements in your career to date?
- Why do you feel you would be successful is this role?
- What are the three attributes that you possess that could add the most value in the position and to the organisation?
- What are your strengths?
- What are your areas of development?
- What would you do in the first six months if you were successful in obtaining this position?
- What are your salary expectations?

- What are you looking for in a company?
- What questions would you like to ask the hiring manager about the position and the organisation?

Stick to responses that are positive, concise and authentic. Be confident in yourself and what you have to offer. Use past examples where possible of when you've added value, contributed ideas, solved problems or achieved great results.

Prepare responses to BDI or STAR questions

Experienced interviewers will use behavioural descriptive interview (BDI) questions or STAR – situation, task, action, result – questions. In doing so, the employer is assessing how well you've handled situations in the past and what outcomes you have achieved. They are not looking for a response that tells them what you *would do* in the situation, but rather what you *have done* in the past. They are first looking to understand if you've encountered a similar situation before, which may be likely to arise in the job that you're interviewing for. They are then looking to see how you've handled the task, what action you took and what the results were.

To prepare, you can develop responses to some of the most common behavioural-based questions, as well as those that you think are most likely to be asked in relation to the job. Here is a list to get you started:

'Please think of an example of a time when you _____.
What was the situation and task, what action did you take and what was the outcome?'

- ... managed a large project
- ... negotiated an important contract
- ... dealt with a difficult customer
- ... influenced a stakeholder
- ... identified an error
- ... faced conflict within a team

... worked with a person whose personality was different to yours
... didn't agree ethically with something that you'd been asked to do
... were given negative feedback
... faced change in your role
... balanced attention to detail with deadlines
... prioritised an overwhelming workload
... used your initiative
... contributed an idea

Behavioural-based interview questions will take many expanded forms and have endless possibilities in terms of situations you could discuss. They will always have the common theme, though, of looking for details of a past situation that you've managed. Preparing in advance to discuss challenging and positive past situations can be helpful in showcasing your skills and experience. Develop a library of key examples that you can bring up during your interview. Even if your interviewer doesn't ask this specific format of behavioural question, you will still have opportunities to talk about key examples. Emphasise key achievements and results that you have delivered.

Develop short- and long-term plans

Imagine you've got the job. What would you do in the first six to twelve months to ensure success? What would you like to achieve in the first three to five years? These might seem like big questions to answer when you haven't even got your feet under the desk, but they might be the exact questions and answers that get you there. You only need high-level dot points, but having these in advance of your interview will be helpful. This is particularly important during a second-stage interview. As an example, let's say you're interviewing to be the Work Health and Safety (WHS) Manager for a medium-sized construction firm. Your first priorities when getting into the job might be:

- reviewing all safety procedures and documentation, and understanding them fully
- building relationships with line managers
- assessing and addressing immediate risks.

Long-term priorities might include:

- reducing onsite injuries through education, appropriate equipment and a healthy workplace culture
- influencing and educating stakeholders on WHS to improve outcomes
- looking at additional ways to improve safety with the lowest commercial impact, while always putting people first.

Look at the position you are interviewing for. Where can you make an immediate impact in the job, and what does this look like long-term? At interview, you'll want the employer to start imagining you in the position achieving outcomes. There's no better way to do this than by communicating your short- and long-term goals if appointed. It shows that you are driven and focussed on outcomes and the impact you can make to the business.

Prepare questions to ask at the end of the interview

When you get to the end of the interview, you'll be offered the opportunity to ask questions. There's nothing less engaging for an interviewer to hear than, 'No, you've answered them all.' Make sure that you come prepared and think outside the box. Basic questions will likely be answered by the interviewer, so prepare questions that demonstrate research, engage the person and get them talking about their business or even themselves. Here are some great examples of questions that follow this format:

> 'Kate, I see you've been working at ABC company for the past five years. What do you love about working here?'

Or:

> 'I noticed on your website that you've just launched a new product. Are you rolling that out primarily in Australia, or internationally too?'

Or:

> 'I love the charity appeal that your company recently got involved in. Is that something that you do a lot of?'

Questions like 'What is the culture like?', 'How many people are in the team?', 'Who does the role report to?' and 'What are the next steps?' are really important questions, but they are likely to be answered upfront by the employer. Ensure that you ask questions that genuinely give you the information that you need, but also engage the interviewer and enhance your chances of moving to the next stage of the recruitment process.

Plan for the day

At least a few days out from the interview, look up the location of where you'll be meeting and understand how long it will take you to get there. Plan your travel for the day and leave plenty of time. Be clear on who you're meeting and who you need to ask for when you arrive. Save to your phone the contact details of the person who has confirmed the interview for you; this can be handy if there are any issues when you get there. Try to arrive at the meeting place ten minutes before your interview. If it makes you feel better to get to the area earlier, you can always enjoy a coffee or some food nearby beforehand. This is a great way to calm your nerves and give you time to review your notes. If your interview is virtual, make sure that you have a link well in advance and a password if required.

Decide what you're going to wear and dress to match the culture of the organisation. Dress just as professionally for a virtual interview as you would for one in person (although you won't be judged for wearing pyjama bottoms, as long as they're out of shot!). You can also ask your recruitment consultant or contact at the organisation what the dress code is. If in doubt, smarter is always better. You want to feel comfortable and confident on the day.

☕ Coffee break

In summary, ahead of your interview, review details, complete documentation and assessments required, and gather your own documents ready to take with you. Undertake thorough research on the company, job, interviewers and competitors, and prepare content for your answers to commonly asked questions. Develop examples that you can use during behavioural interviewing and prepare short- and long-term plans for what you would do if successfully appointed to the role. Prepare engaging questions that demonstrate research and get the interviewer talking. You can also make some plans for the day, including looking up where you're going and deciding how you want to present yourself. Lastly, remember your EVP and career goals from Part I of this book and keep these front-of-mind, along with your key achievements.

With this preparation, you can be confident and composed, knowing that you are well prepared for anything that might come your way.

Chapter 13

Interview with intent

- Excel in virtual and in-person interviews.
- Showcase your achievements, work examples and great results.
- Show an employer why you're the right candidate for the job.

The day is here. It's time to gather your documents, take a deep breath and show how brilliant you are. You arrive early, make your way to reception and take a few deep breaths. You've done all of your preparation. You know everything that there is to know about this company. You've got responses and examples prepared and have even put together a six- and twelve-month plan for the job. You're ready to go. This could be the beginning of the next phase of your career – a job and environment that makes you want to leap out of bed every day.

You've completed your interview preparation and it's time to shine during the meeting. Let's look at how to build rapport from the get-go, demonstrate research, showcase key achievements and highlight examples of great work from your past. You can play to your strengths, address any gaps, be concise and clear, and answer questions directly. You'll want to keep the conversation positive and engaging, and ask lots of great questions. Keeping your EVP front-of-mind, let's explore how to excel on the day.

When you arrive

Leave plenty of time to travel to your destination and arrive in the area early. You can check out the local area, then head to your interview meeting point about ten minutes before the scheduled time. Take a moment to gather your thoughts, revisit your EVP and remind yourself of some key points that you would like to communicate. Follow any sign-in and WHS instructions. If there is a receptionist, greet them in a friendly way and build rapport. I've seen many employers ask their receptionist for an opinion of candidates when they first come in. Were they nice? Friendly? Strike up a conversation about something that you see in reception, such as awards or product information, or simply ask about their day to make a great first impression.

Building rapport and body language

When the employer or recruiter arrives, shake their hand confidently (otherwise a friendly nod is fine if there are WHS concerns, for example COVID-19). Build rapport by asking how the interviewer is or how their day has been. It's a great idea to have an icebreaker in mind such as, 'I noticed the customer service award you have in reception, that's great – was there a particular initiative that helped you win that?' You can immediately show an interest in the company and get the interviewer talking.

Wait until the interviewer sits down before you do too. From a body language perspective, this helps to maintain the balance of power in the room and can indicate that you are equals in the conversation.

Mirror body language where possible so that you can communicate in a style that is comfortable for the interviewer. It's common to become thirsty when you get nervous, so definitely say yes if offered a glass of water, and bring a bottle with you just in case. Be conscious of nervous habits like shaking your leg, saying 'um' a lot or losing your lovely smile. To help with this, you can do a practice interview with a friend or family member and ask for feedback. Remember that you have a lot to offer, so take a few deep breaths, relax, smile and engage with the interviewer – easier said than done, but with practice it can become more natural. You might even enjoy the interview experience!

Using eye contact is a great way to build rapport, as is referencing the person's name throughout the conversation. If there are multiple interviewers, be sure to engage all of them equally. You can also refer to parts of your research; for example, 'Maria, I noticed that you're on the committee for environmental sustainability for your local council; sustainability is also important to me and I love the way that ABC company is furthering initiatives to reduce its carbon footprint'. Referencing information that you could only know from your own research is a great way to show that you have come prepared. It is also flattering for the person you are talking to that you are interested in them and their background, and have noticed the great work the company is doing in a particular area.

If you see something on the wall of the interview room, such as a football jumper, team photo or award, you could take the opportunity to build rapport by asking about it. Showing that you are interested, observant and complimentary will always leave the interviewer with a great impression.

Answering interview questions

It sounds very simple, but the most common mistake I observe when a candidate is nervous is that they don't actually answer the question asked. They are talking, but it's about something else. Listen well, take a second to think of your response and decide how you can respond directly and concisely. You can draw upon the content that you prepared prior to interview and try to showcase your achievements and examples of great work from the past. A good structure for answering 'What would you do?' type questions is to state why you think it's important, what you would do and then give an example of what you've done in the past. Below is an example.

> *How would you manage deadlines in this role?*
> 'I think getting work completed on time and to expectations is important. I would make sure that I had a clear idea of each deadline, plan out the workload in advance and allow for interruptions. A good example of where I have done this in the past is when I had a 5000-word essay due and it was during our busy Christmas period at work. I planned out the essay and scheduled time in my diary to complete the work. Even though I got called in for extra shifts, I still managed to complete the essay on time and receive a distinction mark for it.'

If you are asked behavioural-based questions such as the BDI or STAR questions discussed in Chapter 12, be sure to provide examples like this.

Remain positive with your responses. If you get asked a tricky question – such as about what your weaknesses or areas of development are, or why you left a particular job – answer honestly and concisely, but don't dwell on the negatives. If asked for areas of development, try to talk about what you have learnt since becoming aware of the gap. For example:

> 'I have high expectations of myself and sometimes I can get impatient if others aren't delivering. I have learnt over time to be more focussed on people's strengths, and to be patient and open-minded.'

If you have left an employer in the past because it wasn't a good fit, it's okay to be honest about this. Most interviewers know that there are two sides to every story and that not every employer is a good one. They will be interested in how you handled the situation, and whether you did it respectfully and professionally. It's better to be upfront about past conflict but not to dwell on the negatives. Show that you are able to overcome challenges and move on.

Try to be concise and succinct with your answers. I often see over-answering, with candidates nervously going off on a tangent. It's better to give just enough information to answer the question directly. If the interviewer wants to know more, they can probe further for details. If you spend too long answering one question, they might have to skip other important questions and leave the interview feeling uncertain about your fit for the role. It's also a much more engaging interview style for the person asking the questions. Be authentic with your answers, slow your speech down if nervous, and try to relax and enjoy the experience.

Play to your strengths and communicate with the interviewer what it is that you offer over other candidates. You might have knowledge of a particular software package that will make it less time-consuming for them to train you, or maybe you speak a second language that could be useful to customers. Think about what it is that really makes you stand out, and be confident in selling yourself.

It is true that self-promotion is not natural for everyone, and a lot of candidates that I meet say that they struggle to talk openly about themselves, even feeling embarrassed at times. You may be introverted, or come from a cultural background where self-promotion is not the norm. This can present a challenge at the interview stage, which is the time to showcase your success and achievements. A great way to do this without appearing boastful is to support your statements with S.T.A.R. (situation, task, action, result) examples. You can also acknowledge where you have improved and what you have learnt along the way. This can help to show the humble and human side to your personality. Of course, you can actively promote your EVP, but striking a balance is key: have confidence in your abilities while remaining true to your own values.

Talk about your past experience, but also about what you would do in the job at hand. It's very common for me to see candidates get stuck in their past when answering a question that could actually be future-focussed. If you can get the employer visualising you in the job and understanding how you would handle situations specific to their organisation, they are more likely to see you as forward-thinking. Offer past experience *and* future strategies.

If you are interviewing with a recruitment agency, be open and honest about your true motivations and what you want in a job. Agencies often have multiple positions available and want to help match you to the right job: it's in your best interests and theirs. Be confident in your value when discussing salary, but also take guidance from the recruiter in regard to market salaries so that you don't rule yourself out for a particular job. Your recruitment consultant can also give you advice on what to prepare in advance of your interview with an employer, and how to make a great impression.

What is the interviewer looking for?

When faced with a friendly interviewer, you might wonder what is going through their mind. What are they looking for?

First, employers will assess you based on your technical proficiency for the job. Can you do the tasks required of the role well? It will depend on the requirements of the position which skills, attributes and experience they are looking for. Being able to do the job's tasks is very important, of course, but equally important is what it will be like to work with you. Employers look for several common qualities in any employee, regardless of the position. In addition to your technical proficiency, the interviewer will be looking for these common desirable qualities:

- Friendly nature
- Team player
- Self-motivation
- Honesty
- Attention to detail
- Good listener

- Quick learner
- Curiosity
- Proactivity
- Problem solving
- Confidence
- Resilience
- Drive
- Good communication skills
- Adaptability
- Work ethic
- Loyalty
- Positivity

Employers are looking for people who will be enjoyable to work with and considerate of others, and who will care about teamwork. They will be seeking employees who can be self-directed with their own work and don't need to have someone looking over their shoulder for them to do the right thing. They will seek out attention to detail to ensure that important parts of the job don't slip through the cracks. Good listening skills will help a new employee take in important information, and having a quick learner on board will always be an advantage. A healthy level of curiosity can also drive employees to find out more about particular subjects within their job. Employees who anticipate needs and are proactive in their approach can help minimise issues and drive new initiatives. Applying problem-solving skills also goes a long way to doing a great job.

Hiring someone with confidence in their own abilities in turn gives the employer confidence that their employee can make decisions and have conviction in their actions. The ability to work through challenges and bounce back after setbacks is also appealing. Being driven and showing some level of ambition or desire to learn and improve will also impress the interviewer. They will be looking for good communication skills and adaptability to change. A strong work ethic, reliability and conscientiousness are seen as important traits, as is loyalty to an employer and commitment to deliver over the long term. Lastly and most importantly, employers will seek out positive, upbeat personalities and a 'can do' attitude. Even at managerial levels, positivity and optimism have been proven time and time again to be some of the most important attributes of great leaders.

Think about how you can foster these characteristics in your own career. Some will come naturally to you, and others you might have to work at. Think about ways that you can showcase your alignment with each area during your interview. Give a nod to these characteristics as you share examples and achievements from your past, and present yourself in a positive, friendly and optimistic way. Be true to yourself, but remember what it is that employers seek in every new employee. Developing these characteristics in the long term can certainly further your career.

Communicate key messages

In your interview, communicate your EVP clearly and deliver key messages, such as what you can bring to the job. You can keep the conversation on track by influencing the narrative consciously. Be prepared with examples from your work history where you've delivered great results, and steer the conversation towards what you would do in the role if appointed. This gets the interviewer *imagining you in the job*, rather than *assessing you* for the job. They will be impressed if they can see that you're passionate about the results you can achieve. Show them that you've thought about what's required to hit key goals and that you are ready to go. Seeing that you can 'hit the ground running' will be a huge advantage.

Ask great questions

Prepare questions that are really outside the box. Research thoroughly and demonstrate this in the questions that you ask. If you can get the interviewer talking about themselves, their business or something that they are passionate about, you are definitely on the right track. Your chance to ask questions is usually towards the end of the interview and can often be their last interaction with you on the day. Ensure that they leave feeling that you are interested in them, their company and their interests. This is also your opportunity to decide if you want the job and whether they are the employer for you. Through great questions you can gather information and display your research, attention to detail, passion, listening skills, curiosity, confidence and positivity.

At the end of the interview

If copies of your ID documents or certificates haven't been asked for by this stage, it's a good time to offer to provide them. This can show your proactivity and how prepared you are. It also saves you having to come in and provide them at a later date. You can also leave a copy of your current CV with your interviewer as a reminder of you after the interview. Lastly, if you have a portfolio or examples of work to show, offer them to the interviewer now.

Clarify next steps. Will you expect to receive a call or email? Within what timeframe? If you're successful in progressing to the next stage of the recruitment process, what will this involve? Behavioural profiling? Two or three interviews? A presentation? Knowing now what is coming up can help you to get prepared.

Thank the interviewer for their time and mention something that you really enjoyed about meeting them; for example:

> 'Thanks for your time Phil. I really enjoyed hearing more about ABC company.'

Checklist for a great interview

- Be prepared.
- Build rapport.
- Mirror body language.
- Be succinct.
- Answer the question!
- Showcase examples of work and achievements.
- Show that you can hit the ground running.

- Play to your strengths.
- Talk about what you have done and would do in the role.
- Clarify next steps and thank the interviewer.

Interviewing virtually

Since COVID-19 swept the world in 2020, virtual interviews have become the new normal; you can expect to see a lot more of them in the years to come. If you are asked to a virtual interview, the same advice applies. Make sure that you have a reliable internet connection, good lighting and that your face and shoulders are visible in the meeting view. Have the camera at eye level where possible, and choose a confidential space where you can speak freely and openly. If interviewing from home, ensure that family members and pets are looked after and won't rain on your parade (although most employers are pretty understanding these days). Present yourself professionally, as you would in person. Log into the virtual meeting room about two minutes before your meeting is due to start. This can be helpful when there are sign-in or password requirements. You will usually enter into a waiting area and be let in when the host is ready.

Building rapport is even more important during a virtual interview as some of the spark can get lost in 2D mode. Bring your energy, positivity and enthusiasm to the table and you'll put the interviewer at ease.

Impressing in second-round interviews

You've made it back for a second interview and are getting closer to landing the job. How can you make yourself stand out to the employer and ensure that you will be the one receiving the offer? This is where your six- and twelve-month plan for what you would do in the role becomes really important. You will have gathered more information in the initial interview, and you can now use this to your advantage in preparing a high-level plan. Show what you have learnt from the last interview and the research that you have conducted in between. For some managerial positions, it is even appropriate to bring a short presentation to the interview and show the employer what you would do if hired. You have to strike a balance between giving enough information and also acknowledging respectfully that you have very limited information about the organisation. Avoid conveying that you might come in like a bull in a china shop and instead show your willingness to get to know people within the organisation, understand the existing set-up and enhance current organisational strengths. You can even expand this to a three- or five-year plan. By getting the interviewer focussed on what you would do in the position, you help them imagine you taking the reins successfully. It shows that you are driven, proactive, self-motivated and ready to go.

After the interview

Send a follow-up thank you email to the interviewer to show your appreciation and enthusiasm. Mention something that you really enjoyed about the meeting, such as a fact you learnt about them or the company. Offer any follow-up information requested and let them know that you are looking forward to next steps. If you're interested in pursuing the position further after the first interview, get your referee details ready if you haven't already supplied them. If you don't hear back within two weeks of the interview, it is appropriate to give your recruiter or the employer a call.

Reference checking

When conducting a recruitment process, reference checking is typically completed in the final stages. A good recruiter or prospective employer will ensure that they are speaking with a verified direct manager that you have worked for in the past. They will want to understand your title, dates of employment, duties, how you performed, achievements and any areas for development.

Contact your referees and advise them that they may expect to receive a call from a prospective employer. By giving them advance notice of the call, they won't be caught off-guard, and you can avoid delaying any potential job offers. They can also make time in their diary to answer the questions properly and leave a better impression with the recruiter or employer. Having prior knowledge of the position can assist the referee in tailoring their answers to be relevant to the job. This can ensure that your best skills, experience and qualities are showcased. Maintaining a great relationship with previous employers is an excellent way to prepare for reference checking in the future.

> ### ☕ Coffee break
>
> Prepare thoroughly in advance of your interview and you will be on the right track to a job offer. Leave plenty of time for travel, present yourself professionally and bring required documents along. Build rapport through eye contact, finding common interests and using the interviewer's name throughout. Show that you have done research by mentioning information that you've discovered. Listen carefully to interview questions and answer them directly. Highlight key achievements and examples of situations in the past where you have delivered great results. Be friendly, positive and curious, and play to your strengths. Keep in mind the key qualities that employers look for, and demonstrate these through your responses, great questions and body language. Communicate your EVP and the advantages you bring as a candidate to the role. Thank the interviewer for their time and send a follow-up email. You can also impress in second-round interviews by discussing short- and long-term plans for what you would do in the job. Finally, be confident in your own abilities, sell yourself well and enjoy the experience.
>
> Let's explore job offers further in Chapter 14, and how you can negotiate your employment terms and contract.

Chapter 14

Manage job offers

- Negotiate your salary and know what you're worth.
- Manage employment offers, benefits, hours and conditions.
- Understand contracts and what to look out for.

You've been through several rounds of interviews and completed behavioural profiling, and your referees have been called. The next phone call you get is a job offer. It's exciting and overwhelming, but you're happy to receive the call. When the offer is made, you're pleased with the salary on offer, the conditions and benefits. But of course, you knew what these would be – you'd checked all of this in advance. Thankfully you were prepared, organised and confident in your approach. You're ready to talk about start dates.

The key to receiving a job offer that you're happy with is discussing your preferences earlier in the process. You don't want to be surprised at the point of offer – or worse still, disappointed. It's good to be clear on all elements, such as the duties, tasks, responsibilities, location, hours, reporting lines, team, career progression opportunities, salary and benefits. You can gather a lot of this information through your own research, via your recruitment consultant, or by asking the internal recruiter or line manager directly. Revisit Chapter 3 now to discover what an employer can offer you. Consider all of these elements when researching an organisation and deciding whether you want to work there. Knowing what to ask, where to look and what factors are important to you in your job will be key to being happy at work.

Make sure it's an offer you want to accept

A 2018 study by Mercer found that 39% of employees across many different organisations were planning to leave their current employer. There were many reasons why, including lack of appreciation, burnout, no flexibility, culture, relationships with management, lack of engagement and limited career growth. At people2people we hear many different reasons why candidates are leaving their current job. The main reasons that come up time and time again are poor culture, lack of career development, unhappiness with their manager and job location. It pays to evaluate these elements closely in an employer before making the leap. Here are some great questions to consider ahead of accepting a job offer:

- Does this employer provide flexible and remote working options?
- What are the working hours like, and the approach to work-life balance?
- How do they celebrate success?
- What is the organisational culture like?
- Who is in your proposed team, and what are they like?
- Do you like the manager that you will be reporting to? What is their leadership style?
- Are you happy to travel to the work site regularly?
- What sort of opportunities are there for career development and growth?

Look out for examples of how the organisation has demonstrated this behaviour in the past. For example, when discussing flexibility, the recruiter might give you an example such as, 'We have two employees working fully remotely and three part-time currently'. Hearing about current and past examples shows that the information goes beyond lip-service and has actually been put in place by the organisation.

You'll notice that 'salary increase' didn't come up at all in the reasons listed above. This is because it is very rarely the driving factor in a person changing jobs. Sure, it can be a nice addition if it happens, but an employee is much more likely to change jobs due to the other reasons listed earlier. Salary is important, though, so let's explore how to negotiate it well.

Negotiating your salary

To inform your salary discussion, conduct research using publicly available salary guides, job boards and share-and-compare websites such as salarysiite.com.au. Most large recruitment agencies will publish a salary guide each year, giving you a range that relates to your specific profession. This is often broken down into years of experience too. It's important to consider the specific skills, experience and education that you bring to the job. A first-year lawyer may be at the bottom of the tier-one salary range, while a candidate with five years' experience might be at the top of that tier or somewhere in the one above.

How in-demand your skills and experience are can influence salary too. The term 'UX designer' – short for 'user experience designer' – was coined in 1993, but it wasn't until 2015 that it became an in-demand job across the world. Suddenly everyone wanted a UX designer, and very few candidates had the appropriate skills or experience. In the early days of this demand frenzy, we saw the salaries of UX Designer candidates skyrocket. But less than three years later, salaries started to track downwards, as many experienced candidates entered the market. The same happened for digital marketers and social media managers, and many other jobs. Over the last century, as skilled professions like lamplighting and typesetting disappeared, new jobs appeared, such as podcast producing, app developing and AI chat bot copywriting. If the skills of a new job were hard to find, the salary would go up. So, if your skills are in high demand, then you may have more leverage when it comes to discussing salary. You can get a sense of this by how frequently jobs are advertised online, and by reviewing job demand research from online job boards and via government websites such as joboutlook.gov.au.

In your salary discussion, it's important to consider employer expectations. The manager of an employee on a $55K package may have lower expectations than the manager of an employee on a $90K package. It's important to strike a 'win-win' salary agreement – one which works for both you *and* the employer. If employer expectations are too high, then your job may become stressful. On the flip side, you don't want to be doing a job for less than you should be earning, so getting the balance right is key.

If you're working with a recruitment agency, you may be asked about your current and previous salaries and your expectations. It's important to be upfront and honest with this information so that the recruitment consultant can negotiate a good offer for you. Your salary history may also be checked with your referees. Conduct research prior to having this conversation to ensure that your salary expectations are reasonable and fair for the proposed job. Your recruitment consultant can also give you a guide about salaries in the market. They will negotiate salary on your behalf, ensuring that it is a win-win solution for both you and the employer. It helps no-one if you are underpaid, because then you aren't likely to stay in the job very long. Your recruitment consultant may advise that you're able to ask for a higher salary, or manage your expectations if your requested salary is too high. Overpitching your salary can price you out of job discussions or reveal whether the job is right for you.

When your recruitment consultant negotiates your salary, they will manage the employer's expectations and offer before it reaches you. For example, if the employer offers a $65K package but the recruitment consultant believes that the market rate for your skills and experience is a $70K package, then they will likely ask the employer to reconsider their offer before they present it to you. This benefits the employer too, as they are more likely to gain a loyal, long-term employee who feels fairly rewarded for their skills and experience. Internal recruitment consultants use a similar process to recruitment agencies and will often advocate for you in regard to fair pay when discussing with line managers.

If you are negotiating your salary directly with the employer, ensure that you have conducted thorough research into pay rates. There may or may not be a salary listed on the job advertisement if you have applied via a job board. Be clear about your desired base and other benefits where applicable, such as a bonus structure. However, show the employer that you are flexible in your approach to salary and open to a discussion. This allows you to stay in the recruitment process longer to gather more information about the job, company, team, management, environment and benefits. Once you have all of the information you need and are clear on what's required in the job, then you can confirm your preferred salary. Here's an example discussion regarding salary and what questions you might be asked:

Employer/Recruiter:	'Felicia what is your current salary?'
Candidate:	'I'm on $60K plus superannuation and commission.'
Employer/Recruiter:	'Great, and what salary are you looking for?'
Candidate:	'I'm ideally seeking $65K plus superannuation and commission, but I'm flexible in regard to this.'

Avoid sudden tune changes late in the recruitment process. If your salary expectations have changed, be sure to let the recruiter or employer know early in the piece and do your research as soon as possible. Salary surprises are not received well at later stages of the recruitment process and may mean that other candidates miss out on the job if you have taken up an interview place.

You may be asked about a *hypothetical* offer during the recruitment process. Recruitment consultants often ask this question after the first or second interview to help address any concerns that the candidate might have. They might say, 'We've spoken about the salary being $65K plus superannuation. Hypothetically, if they did offer you the job, would you accept?' If your answer is a resounding 'yes' then the recruiter might say, 'Great, is there anything else you would like to know about the job, or do you have any questions?' If your answer is 'maybe' or 'I'm not sure' then the recruitment consultant will ask you further questions to determine what information you would like, to help you make a decision. They are unlikely to put an offer forward to you if you are undecided about the job. They will ensure that all of your questions have been answered first and then put an offer to you.

Lastly, when negotiating your salary, ensure that you are clear about the details. Does the amount quoted include superannuation, KiwiSaver or a pension amount? Is the superannuation statutory or do they pay more in addition? Is there a bonus or commission structure? If yes, how do you qualify for it and what goals do you need to meet? Finally, be clear on the benefits package on offer. At this stage you don't want to appear overly focussed on the benefit details, but it is certainly nice to have a high-level view. Benefits may include extra parental leave or pay, extra annual leave, wellness initiatives, subsidised food or gym memberships, access to product discounts, included dry cleaning, health insurance, car or car allowance, and more.

How to handle the offer conversation

If you have conducted thorough research prior to a job offer being made and decided whether you want the job or not, then you should hopefully be in a good position to accept it with confidence. This can give the employer certainty and helps get the relationship off to a good start. Think about the awkwardness of a marriage proposal being met with, 'Can I think about it?' Getting a job offer is much the same. Give the employer a sense of your enthusiasm by being fully prepared for an offer to be extended.

Getting the salary right

Of course, there may be the odd situation where the employer's offer is underwhelming and doesn't meet expectations. If you think the offer isn't right, you can either reject it or ask for a revision. For example, you might say:

> 'John, thank you so much for the offer. I'm very excited that you are happy to have me as part of the team. In regard to salary, we had discussed a $70,000 package. I noticed that the salary on offer is now a $65,000 package. Is there any reason for the change?'

At this point the employer may notice an error at their end, or they may give an explanation. Depending on the reasoning, you may choose to accept the new offer or ask something like:

> 'Would it be possible to look at increasing the salary to a $70,000 package please? I have a few other positions that I'm looking at currently. This one is my preference, but it would be great if we could please revisit the salary.'

It's important to discuss any concerns that you have now, before a contract is prepared.

Asking for flexibility

If flexibility, hours, part-time employment or working from home are important to you, be sure to raise this with your prospective employer now. Enquire about the company's flexibility and work-from-home policy first. They may already offer what you are looking for. If you need to negotiate outside of this, don't be afraid to request something different, as long as you can get your job done well and make it work for the employer too. Consider other team members and how flexibility impacts them as well. Most organisations now offer flexible working, and tools and resources to support you with it, as long as you can achieve what's required in your role. Be open and discuss it early in the recruitment process, then confirm details during the offer conversation to avoid any surprises when you start.

Finalise details

Agree on a start date, working hours and location, and ask about what the training and induction process looks like. You can clarify dress code, what equipment will be provided and ask if there is anything that you need to prepare ahead of your start date. Ask when you are likely to receive your contract and what information they need from you to prepare it. You may also ask about receiving a payroll form and any other onboarding documentation. At the end of the call, thank the employer for the opportunity, convey your enthusiasm in joining the team and agree on when you'll speak next.

What to look out for in the contract

Once you receive your employment contract, it's a great idea to seek independent legal advice. Give your lawyer advance warning that you might be sending it over so that there are no delays to you reviewing, signing and returning it to your new employer. If you are not able to access legal advice for financial or personal reasons, there are a few things that you'll want to ensure are in order in the contract.

Position details

Employers usually have a standard employment contract that they adapt for each position. They make variations by attaching a schedule which lists the position, salary, start date, benefits, and other information like location, hours of work or commission structure details. Commission or bonus structures are often referenced in the schedule, stating whether you're eligible, but full structure details tend to be documented outside of the employment contract as they can be subject to change. Ensure that all details listed are correct and align with what has been discussed during the verbal offer.

Probation period

Most organisations have a probation period for permanent employment, during which employment can be terminated with a small amount of notice. This is the period of time when the employer and employee can assess whether there is a good fit between the company, the employee and the job. Probation periods are usually three to six months in length; any longer than that is worth being reviewed by a lawyer or someone experienced that you trust.

Restraint periods

Restraint periods are common for employees who have access to clients and have close relationships with them. Restraints are often put in place to allow the organisation to introduce a new contact to clients when an employee leaves. It is often a fair exchange for the investment that the company will make in your training, development, salary and resources to support you. It gives the organisation the time it needs to resume client relationships, and often prevents you from soliciting business from previous clients for a period of time or approaching employees about jobs. Common restraint periods are three to six months for non-managerial employees, or six to twelve months for managers. The geographical area is usually limited to the city or state that you work in, rather than the entire country. Get a second opinion on the contract if the restraint terms are broader than this.

Additional sections

You will likely see clauses to protect confidential information and intellectual property. Generally, any content or material that you develop on company time is owned by the organisation if this is stated within the employment contract. There may be a clause relating to termination of your employment. Ensure that fair and adequate notice periods are included and available to both the employer and to you. There will usually be a reference to which state or country law governs the agreement and clauses related to severability, and how terms can be varied – usually in writing. There is often a statement regarding the entire agreement and that other conversations or discussions, whether written or verbal, cannot be relied upon. If this is the case, ensure all important information that has been discussed during your verbal offer *is* included in your contract.

Lastly, there will be a signing page. Once you are happy with everything contained in the agreement, you can sign the contract in the presence of a witness and send it back to your employer.

☕ Coffee break

When managing your job offer, come to the table prepared, researched and clear on whether you would except an offer and under what conditions. Consider in advance what an employer can offer you and the benefits that you are looking for. Look at demand, expectations and salary guides before approaching the conversation. Give clarity on what your preferences are, but also offer flexibility in your approach and allow yourself to gather key information throughout the recruitment process. If offered a job, check that it matches what was previously discussed, clarify details and provide your response. Handle negotiation delicately, reinforcing how pleased you are that they are interested in you for the job. In the contract, look at position details, probation periods and restraint details, and seek independent legal advice where possible. Managing the job offer process well can get your relationship with your new employer off to a great start. Enhance it further by learning in the next chapter how to set yourself up for success.

Chapter 15

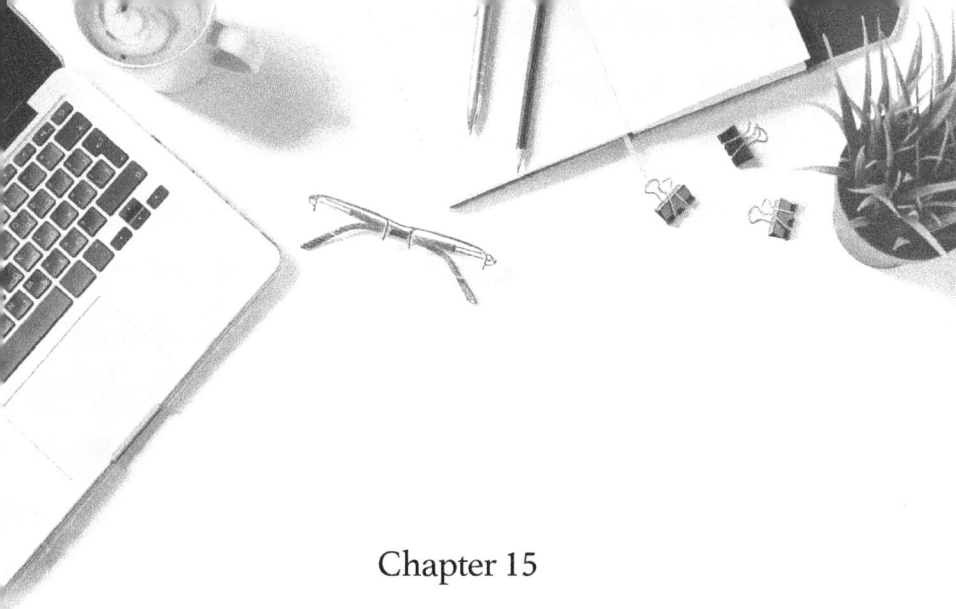

Set yourself up for success

- Make a great first impression in your new job.
- Know what to expect during your induction and onboarding.
- Understand career currency and how to set yourself up for success.

You got the job! You got the job you *really* wanted. Congratulations. It's a big achievement. It's been a long process of preparation, job searching, interviews, assessments and negotiating. You've put in a lot of hard work, and it has paid off. Now it's time to set yourself up for success in your new job, build relationships, learn systems and processes, and undertake some goal-setting.

A 2014 study showed that loyalty and attitudes towards work are significantly influenced by an employer's induction program. Employees are more likely to stay long-term and have a higher level of commitment to their work if the new employee induction program is good. Just as your organisation's induction program might influence your view of the company, so too can the first interactions that you have with your colleagues and managers influence *their* view of you. During your induction you have a great opportunity to meet stakeholders, establish relationships, understand the organisation thoroughly and show what sort of personality, work ethic, experience and skills you bring to the table. First impressions matter, and during the induction period is when you can make a great impression. Let's explore what to expect during your first few weeks in your new job and how you can set yourself up for success.

Induction and onboarding – what to expect

An induction is your initial interaction with your new company, when you are familiarised with the organisation, your position and what's expected of you. Onboarding can take much longer – weeks, months or even a year – and encompasses all training required to bring you up to speed in relation to your job.

On your first day, you are likely to be introduced to people in your immediate team, be given a tour of the office or site and taken through an initial introduction to the company. This may cover the organisation's mission, vision, values and goals. You may be asked to complete a WHS induction and be trained on any key safety equipment such as fire extinguishers, the location of first-aid kits and emergency procedures. If there is any outstanding paperwork, such as a witnessed contract of employment or policies that need to be reviewed and signed, then this is often completed on your first morning. Employers usually explain policies in detail before you are required to sign and agree to them.

You'll get to meet key people within the business that you will be working with, such as colleagues, your manager and any other key stakeholders that you may liaise or work with on a regular basis – like human resources team members or the executive leadership team. Your manager will give you an overview of your job, set expectations regarding your tasks and duties, and outline what success looks like in the position. They may assess any skill gaps and training needs, and put a plan in place to address them. A good manager will also ask you about your goals within the organisation and what you'd like to learn and achieve while in the role. This is your opportunity to show your ambition and the thoroughness of your research, and articulate what is important to you in your job.

Your company may provide you with an overview of your first week and what to expect during your training period. Training may include education on systems, processes, products, services, company structure, competitors, customers and core duties. You may be asked to view training online, in person, in a classroom-based setting, one to one or in group scenarios. As you progress through your training, you are likely to have tasks to complete between training sessions, and will begin to familiarise yourself with your new environment, colleagues and the duties of your position.

Making a great first impression

Building relationships is key to making a great first impression. You can get off on the right foot by conducting research prior to your first day. Look up your manager online, particularly on LinkedIn. What background do they have and what sort of worldview might they hold? You can research colleagues, senior executives and other key stakeholders. Knowing something about your colleagues and managers before starting your job can show that you are prepared, conscientious, respectful and enthusiastic. You can build rapport by mentioning something you've noticed about them, such as 'Yes, I see you're managing the polymers division, is that right?' or, 'I saw that you've been here five years. Great to meet you.' People are likely to be flattered that you've taken an interest in them and that you care about who you are working with.

When meeting with your manager for the first time, come prepared with a list of questions that you would like to ask during your induction. Many of your questions will be answered straight away, but asking additional questions can help you stay informed and show that you are interested, keen to learn, curious and proactive. Be clear on what you want to achieve while in the role and what support you would like from your manager to help you get there. Knowing this in advance can help you to make a great impression, showing that you are focussed and achievement-oriented. Familiarise yourself with the organisation's values and any company or product information online, and come prepared. During training sessions, be an active participant by taking lots of notes and asking great questions.

Career planning

You just got a new job, right? Why would we talk about career planning now? Well, it's the perfect time to do it. You will never have a cleaner slate within a new business to write the script that you want to see play out during your time working there. You can come in and go with the flow, or you can set some goals, make a plan and work towards what you would like to achieve. Ensure that your goals are aligned with your organisation's goals and you are likely to be rewarded with an enjoyable job and work environment.

How do you go about this planning process? Use the following roadmap to assist you. First, revisit your career goals from Chapter 1 and adjust them if they have changed. Then ask yourself the following questions:

✏️ CAREER PLAN ROADMAP

12-month plan:

1. What would I like to achieve in this position in the next 12 months?

_____

_____

_____

_____

2. What action do I need to take to make that happen?

_____

_____

_____

3. What support, training or resources do I need from my manager or organisation to get there?

_____

_____

_____

Five-year plan:

1. Where would I like to be in my career in five (or ten) years' time?

_____

_____

_____

2. What action do I need to take to make that happen?

_____

_____

_____

3. What support, training or resources do I need from my manager or organisation to get there?

_____

_____

_____

To underpin your twelve month and five-year plans, list specific goals that you would like to achieve within the time period; for example, 'Achieving an advanced level of reporting skills within

MYOB' or 'Developing my leadership skills'. Then list what you need to do to get there, such as 'Familiarising myself with the MYOB help section and using it frequently' or 'Undertaking a leadership training course and leading by example'. Finally, list any support, training or resources your organisation can provide. Having clarity on what you would like to achieve within the organisation and within your career can keep you focussed on achievements, goals and progress.

It's a great idea to communicate your goals with your manager early on in your new job and collaborate on ways that you can work towards them. This approach is usually seen as proactive, forward-thinking and outcome-focussed – all very positive traits in a new employee. By doing this you may also find yourself a 'sponsor' within the organisation. This is someone who can advocate for you at more senior levels and with existing employees, and who can support your career direction and professional development.

Career currency

As you move through the process of career planning, think of your career options as if they have a price tag on them. You are going to purchase your ideal job with currency: *career* currency. Career currency is essentially the value that you can offer an employer. The amount of career currency you have in the bank is influenced by several factors, including your skills, experience, education, achievements, industry exposure, relationships that you can bring with you, and your personality and attitude. But there is one factor that influences career currency more than anything else in your bid for the right job. It's not your achievements, although they are important. It's not where you went to school or who you know. It's not which companies you have worked for or what promotions you've had. It's this: *Loyalty*.

Loyalty gets you noticed. Loyalty gets you double, triple or even quadruple your money's worth in the world of career currency. You can have all the achievements in the world, and the best attitude and skills, but they are worth very little to an employer if you are not willing to stick around long enough for your employer to see a return on investment. It takes months, sometimes years, for an employer to receive a return on the skills and experience you bring to the table. And in that time, they are training you, investing in your salary and supporting you with resources. So if you leave in a short period of time, it actually *costs* the employer money.

I often hear candidates say, 'I wish I hadn't left XYZ company' and observe on their CV a series of short-lived positions after a five-, ten- or twenty-year stint at a company that they really loved. They spend years looking for that same enjoyment again. The grass isn't always greener, so choose your jobs wisely. Think carefully before you make the leap. Ask all the questions you need, meet your potential team and see the environment with your own eyes. If you choose an employer that you really want to work for and a job that you love, then you can offer loyalty, enhance your career currency and build your career in the process.

Mindset for success and enjoyment

Starting a new job is daunting, but research, planning and goal-setting can take the edge off. Your mindset can also make a huge difference. If you are excited about the opportunity, the company, the people and the potential to grow within the organisation, then your first few days can certainly fly by.

When assisting with career planning, I always advise individuals to visualise themselves in the job they want to have in five years' time. What does it feel like? Look like? Sound like? How are you behaving? Do people respect you? Do they like you and enjoy working with you? Visualise that now and decide who you want to show up as today. If you have aspirations to become a manager one day, you can behave like one now. That doesn't mean showing up to work and bossing everyone around. It means leading by example, being a team player, communicating clearly, showing empathy and demonstrating a positive work ethic. If you have aspirations to be a subject-matter expert, keep yourself up to date and seek out learning opportunities. And if you would like to advocate for an important cause, demonstrate the behaviour that gains the credibility you need to have a genuine voice. Now is the time to adopt that behaviour. Now is the time to be the person that you want to be – the future you.

☕ Coffee break

When setting yourself up for success in your new job, conduct research beforehand and walk into your first day feeling confident. Make a great first impression by building relationships with colleagues, managers and key stakeholders. Convey enthusiasm and willingness to learn by actively participating in training and induction sessions. Prepare a career plan and set goals to achieve in your new job. Visualise yourself in five years' time: Who do you want to be? How do you want people to perceive you? Do you aspire to leadership or technical expert status, or to make a difference to the environment or other people's lives? Enhance your career currency by being strategic with your career choices and showing loyalty to employers who are willing to invest in you. In your new role, you have the potential to do a great job, to make your mark, to stretch and challenge yourself, to support and encourage others and to make a difference.

Remember the career goals you set back in Chapter 1? Keep them firmly in mind. It's possible that with determination and focus, you can hit your career goals in the future – or perhaps some other attractive path will reveal itself along the way. Either way, having a plan will keep you outcome-focussed, achieving and progressing in your career – and hopefully enjoying yourself *a lot* along the way!

You're valuable, you're worth it, and you deserve a great job.
Don't just get a job.
Get the job you *really* want!

For up-to-date advice on careers, recruitment and employment, connect with Erin on social media:

- linkedin.com/in/erindevlin
- @erin_devlin_
- @erin_devlin

Thank you

There are so many people to thank for making this book happen. Too many, in fact, to mention here.

Firstly, to my baby boys, Will and Alex – for going without their mummy on weekends and for always asking me in their sweet two-year-old voices, 'Did you write your book, Mummy?', closely followed by encouraging shouts of, 'Well done, Mummy!' Your beautiful personalities helped inspire me to write this book for everyone willing to 'give it a go'. I wish you a future that is bright, fulfilling and, most of all, fun!

To my husband, Tom – for being the most amazing father to our twin boys Will and Alex, and for providing me with endless support throughout the writing of this book. You've sacrificed many hours to help me make this happen. Your honest, clear feedback and advice on the book's ideas and design have been invaluable.

To my parents, Neva and Craig – for always encouraging me to 'go for it', supporting me in reaching my goals, and showing me that the possibilities in life are endless. Mum, your support with Will and Alex while I have been busy writing means the world. You've shown them that kindness, manners, having fun and giving it a go are everything when you're a toddler.

Dad, thank you for your sage business advice and suggestions for enlightening quotes and additions in just the right places in chapters of this book. You provided some early advice regarding structure and I've followed this to a tee.

To my gorgeous sister Shona – for being my number-one cheerleader and inspiration. Your positive, exuberant approach to life is infectious. You've spurred me on to speak my mind and be a leader even when it has taken lots of courage. Thank you for opening my mind, challenging my views and being a constant source of encouragement and light in my life.

To my nieces, Austin and Neave, and my nephew, Huxley – thank you for being an inspiration for this book, too. You are kind, thoughtful, energetic and full of brilliant ideas. I think about your futures and hope that they are fulfilling, meaningful and make you happy every day.

To Rachel Lucas – for your brilliant, honest and indispensable advice on the CV chapters. I have been so lucky to have your view as an experienced executive search consultant and another source of encouragement for this book as a family member.

To Lesley Williams, my publisher, and her amazing team at Major Street Publishing. Thank you for approaching me with this opportunity and for providing clear feedback, advice and honesty along the way. Your years of experience are what have helped to make this book a pleasure to write.

To Greg Savage – for introducing me to Lesley and for bringing this book opportunity to me, and for making my recruitment career what it is today. You have mentored, supported and encouraged me along the way. You've called me out when I needed it, and raised me up to believe in myself in challenging moments. You've advised me during the hard times and helped celebrate in the good times. You're the reason my recruitment business merged with people2people and why I've had an exhilarating, fulfilling and wildly enjoyable adventure ever since.

To Mark Smith – for throwing your support behind this project and for always having an infinite mindset. You see the world as having abundant opportunity and very few limitations. I find that incredibly inspiring. Thank you for always seeing the light in every situation, keeping a smile on people's faces, and showing leadership and innovation at every turn. You don't build a $100+ million business from scratch without being some sort of brilliant, and you did that with people2people. You're a true leader in every sense and it's why people follow you.

To Charles Cameron – it would be hard to meet anyone more passionate about the recruitment industry and doing right by job seekers than you. Your energetic and infectious personality, and incredible depth of knowledge, are why recruitment leaders across Australia and New Zealand – and indeed the world – have rallied to make recruitment a sought-after profession and to support candidates across the globe. Charles, thank you for providing the foreword for this book and for much advice during its writing, particularly for the 'Recruitment Agencies' chapter and information about different types of employment.

To Will Allen – my editor. Thank you for reworking parts of this book for better flow and setting me straight on comma use. Your eye for detail is incredible and definitely much appreciated.

Thank you to Simone Geary for the lovely cover design, and to Kerry Milin and Production Works for the brilliant internal design. And to all of the sales, marketing and retail teams and bookstores that have helped with promotion – thank you.

To Justine Whipper, who provided content regarding career transition for professional athletes. Your energy and passion for the players that you work with are inspiring. You've helped so many individuals, including job seekers, over the years and made a real difference in their lives.

To Shannon O'Malley – for the comprehensive feedback you provided me with after reading the book and for spending hours over FaceTime debriefing me on edits while I did laps around the neighbourhood (in an attempt to get some exercise in between gigs). Shannon, I have you to thank for helping me produce the worksheets and put ideas into a more structured, digestible format.

Thank you for encouraging me to put more of 'me' into the book and for surveying almost everyone you came into contact with for a few weeks on the title. You've brought a unique academic perspective and shown how this resource could be useful in high school and university settings. Your genuine care for others, incredible maturity, resilience and fun-loving nature are truly inspiring, and have not only shaped parts of this book but also influenced our boys Will and Alex.

To Liz Bernardin – for providing a unique 'recent graduate' perspective on certain aspects of the book and words of encouragement. Your energy, style and enthusiasm are brilliant, and it's no wonder much of that has rubbed off on our boys in the time that they have been lucky enough to spend with you.

To Emilia Corea – for providing endless love and care to our boys during the writing of this book, and for being an ear to listen as I recounted the number of words I had written that day, or the challenges I faced as I wrote and re-wrote aspects. You provided a unique Millennial view on many topics and helped steer me in the right direction for what readers might like.

To Grzegorg Gozdz and Jaime Laird – for giving advice on the cover design, title and topic, and being part of my 'inner circle' along with Ben and Cian.

To my extended family, for being a source of inspiration for this book. To the Devlins and the Archers, thank you for your constant encouragement and for checking in at every turn.

To my late grandparents Betty and Clive Devlin and Laurel Phillips for our secret chats while I was growing up about what exciting things I was planning next. 'That's great, pet' was almost always what I needed to hear to keep me feeling confident and sure that I was heading in the right direction.

To my late Uncle Eric – thank you for being an endless source of interesting facts, intelligent deep dives and exploration into different aspects of the world, and for making me hand-write you letters from the Middle East (even though I found out later that you had a smartphone and an iPad well before anyone else).

To my girlfriends, particularly Jessica Gourley, Leanne Thompson, Alisa Imfeld, Melinda Cox, Natasha McAuley, Ange Cohen and my Strathy girls who have supported me along the way.

To my brilliant people2people team, particularly Liz, Ryan, Mary, Zara, Aimee, Kellie, Krystal and Jess, who have been cheering me on. And to Simon, Manda, Remi, Mark and all of the people2people leadership team, who very quietly have been a source of inspiration and support for me over the past six years.

To our amazing clients and candidates at people2people Recruitment. You are the source of inspiration for this book. Without you, it would not have been possible. You have taught me so much about business, careers, success and life. Thank you for your endless generosity, inspiration and support.

To those who have read or are reading this book, thank you for diving in. I hope it gives you the launchpad for a fabulous career, an enjoyable life and a very successful future.

References and resources

Chapter 1

Bureau of Labor Statistics, *Number of jobs, labor market experience, and earnings growth: results from a national longitudinal survey*, U.S. Department of Labor, 22 August 2019, viewed 15 February 2021 <bls.gov/news.release/pdf/nlsoy.pdf>.

G T Doran, 'There's a S.M.A.R.T. way to write management's goals and objectives', *Management Review*, vol. 70, issue 11, 1981, pp. 35–36.

Chapter 2

Collins English dictionary, HarperCollins Publishers, Glasgow, 1994.

Chapter 3

State of the American workplace, Gallup, 2017, pp. 17 & 71.

V Hunt, D Layton & S Prince, 'Why diversity matters', McKinsey & Company, 1 January 2015, viewed 3 March 2021, <mckinsey.com/business-functions/organization/our-insights/why-diversity-matters>.

M Lyons, K Lavelle & D Smith, *Gen Z rising*, US edition, Accenture, 2017, p. 3.

Small business counts: Small business in the Australian economy, Australian Small Business and Family Enterprise Ombudsman, 2016.

Chapter 4

About LinkedIn, LinkedIn, viewed 15 February 2021 <about.linkedin.com>.

Chapter 5

L Salm, '70% of employers are snooping candidates' social media profiles', CareerBuilder, 15 June 2017, viewed 15 February 2021, <careerbuilder.com/advice/social-media-survey-2017>.

A M Wood, P A Linley, J Maltby, M Baliousis & S Joseph, 'The authentic personality: A theoretical and empirical conceptualization and the development of the Authenticity Scale', *Journal of Counseling Psychology*, vol. 55, issue 3, 2008, pp. 385–399.

E Arens, 'The best times to post on social media in 2020', Sprout Social, 3 August 2020, viewed 15 February 2021 <sproutsocial.com/insights/best-times-to-post-on-social-media/>.

Chapter 6

L Eleftheriou-Smith, 'Employers sifting through applications likened to swiping through Tinder as research shows people spend 8.8 seconds looking at a CV', *Independent*, 19 January 2015, viewed 15 February 2021 <independent.co.uk/news/uk/home-news/employers-sifting-through-applications-likened-swiping-through-tinder-research-shows-people-spend-8-8-seconds-looking-cv-9988512.html>.

Chapter 7

Z Liberman, A L Woodward & K D Kinzler, 'The origins of social categorization', *Trends in cognitive sciences*, vol. 21, issue 7, 2017.

D Purnama, 'ValueMyCV: Aussie jobseekers fail the spell test', Adzuna, 20 June 2017, viewed 15 February 2021 <adzuna.com.au/blog/2017/06/20/valuemycv-aussie-jobseekers-fail-spell-test/>.

Chapter 8

M Richardson, 'The earliest business letters in English: An overview', *International Journal of Business Communication*, vol. 17, issue 3, 1980.

Chapter 9

K Chakrabarti, 'How long does it take to get a job in America today? 84.3 days for HR...', TalentWorks, 22 September 2017, viewed 15 February 2021 <talent.works/2017/09/22/how-long-does-it-take-to-get-a-job-60-days-if-youre-in-hr-or-sales/>.

B Turczynski, '2021 HR statistics: job search, hiring, recruiting & interviews', Zety, 8 February 2021, viewed 15 February 2021 <zety.com/blog/hr-statistics>.

J l'Anson, 'How to find unadvertised jobs', *The Guardian*, 23 November 2012, viewed 15 February 2021 <theguardian.com/careers/careers-blog/how-to-find-unadvertised-jobs>.

L Adler, 'New survey reveals 85% of all jobs are filled via networking', LinkedIn, 29 February 2016, viewed 15 February 2021 <linkedin.com/pulse/new-survey-reveals-85-all-jobs-filled-via-networking-lou-adler/>.

The Australian recruitment industry: A comparison of service delivery, Australian Government Department of Employment, 2016.

Statista Research Department, 'Staffing and recruiting industry market size in the United States from 2012 to 2019, with a forecast until 2021', Statista, 28 January 2021, viewed 15 February 2021 <statista.com/statistics/873648/us-staffing-industry-market-size/>.

'Recruitment industry took in a record £38.9 billion despite a difficult year', Recruitment and Employment Confederation (REC), 23 January 2020, viewed 15 February 2021 <rec.uk.com/our-view/news/press-releases/recruitment-industry-took-record-389-billion-despite-difficult-year>.

'It's possible to give personalised feedback to every job applicant', PredictiveHire, viewed 15 February 2021 <predictivehire.com/blog/candidates-personalised-feedback/>.

Chapter 10

K Scott, '8 surprising facts about how we spend our time', ABC, 13 September 2018, viewed 15 February 2021 <abc.net.au/everyday/surprising-facts-about-how-we-spend-our-time/10188202>.

The Australian recruitment industry: A comparison of service delivery, Australian Government Department of Employment, 2016.

2017 Talent Acquisition Benchmarking Report, Society for Human Resource Management (SHRM), 2017.

Agency/Labour Hire, #workingsooner, viewed 15 February 2021 <workingsooner.com.au/agency-labour-hire>.

#loveyourwork, viewed 15 February 2021 <loveyourworkanz.org>.

Chapter 11

'In appreciation: Paul E. Meehl', Association for Psychological Science (APS), 22 July 2003, viewed 15 February 2021 <psychologicalscience.org/observer/in-appreciation-paul-e-meehl>.

S Srivastava, O John, S D Gosling & J Potter, 'Development of personality in early and middle adulthood: Set like plaster or persistent change?', *Journal of Personality and Social Psychology*, vol. 84, issue 5, 2003, pp. 1041–1053.

La la land, motion picture, Summit Entertainment, Los Angeles, 2016.

Chapter 14

2018 global talent trends study: Unlocking growth in the human age, Mercer, 2018.

Chapter 15

O P Salau, H O Falola, J O Akinbode, 'Induction and staff attitude towards retention and organizational effectiveness', *IOSR Journal of Business and Management*, vol. 16, issue 4, 2014, pp. 47–52.

Useful websites

Chapter 1

Career Development Association of Australia – cdaa.org.au
Career Industry Council of Australia – cica.org.au/resources
European Commission – Career Development – euraxess.ec.europa.eu/career-development
Future Ready – schooltowork.dese.gov.au
Job Outlook – joboutlook.gov.au
My Future – myfuture.edu.au
National Career Development Association (USA) – ncda.org/aws/ncda/pt/sp/resources/
National Careers Institute – myskills.gov.au
National Skills Commission – nationalskillscommission.gov.au
Your Career – yourcareer.gov.au

Chapter 3

99designs – 99designs.com.au
Australian Apprenticeships – australianapprenticeships.gov.au
Australian Business Register – abr.gov.au
Fair Work Ombudsman – fairwork.gov.au
Freelancer – freelancer.com.au
GradAustralia – gradaustralia.com.au
TaskRabbit – taskrabbit.com
U.S. Department of Labor – dol.gov
Upwork – upwork.com

Chapter 4

Facebook – facebook.com
LinkedIn – linkedin.com

Chapter 5
Social media sites
Architizer – architizer.com
Buzznet – buzznet.com
Care2 – care2.com
Classmates – classmates.com
Discord – discord.com
Elpha – elpha.com
Facebook – facebook.com
Flickr – flickr.com
Instagram – instagram.com
LinkedIn – linkedin.com
Meetup – meetup.com
Nextdoor – nextdoor.com
Pinterest – pinterest.com
PopBase – pop-base.com
Quora – quora.com
Reddit – reddit.com
ReverbNation – reverbnation.com
Snapchat – snapchat.com
Spreely – spreely.com
StartupNation – startupnation.com
TankChat – tankchat.com
TikTok – tiktok.com
Triller – triller.co
Tumblr – tumblr.com
Twitter – twitter.com
Upstream – upstreamapp.com
WT.Social – wt.social
YouTube – youtube.com
Yubo – yubo.live

Other sites
ABC – abc.net.au
BBC – bbc.com

Buffer – buffer.com
CuePrompter – cueprompter.com
The Economist – economist.com
Followerwonk – followerwonk.com
Forbes – forbes.com
Hootsuite – hootsuite.com
HuffPost – huffpost.com
TweetDeck – tweetdeck.twitter.com

Chapter 6

Lists of associations and business groups

Australian Chamber of Commerce and Industry – australianchamber.com.au
Directory of Associations (USA) – directoryofassociations.com
European Consumer Centre for Services (Europe and UK) – ukecc-services.net

Online portfolio websites

Adobe Portfolio – portfolio.adobe.com
Crevado – crevado.com
Flickr – flickr.com
Journo – Portfolio journoportfolio.com
Muck Rack – muckrack.com/journalists
Portfoliobox – portfoliobox.net
Squarespace – squarespace.com
Wix – wix.com
WordPress – wordpress.com

Chapter 9

Government job support websites

Disability Employment Services – servicesaustralia.gov.au/individuals/topics/disability-employment-services/51421
Jobactive – jobsearch.gov.au
Services Australia – servicesaustralia.gov.au

Work Assist – servicesaustralia.gov.au/individuals/topics/work-assist/51422

Job boards

CareerBuilder (US) – careerbuilder.com
Indeed – indeed.com
Jobactive – jobsearch.gov.au
LinkedIn – linkedin.com/jobs
Monster – monster.com
REED (UK) – reed.co.uk
SEEK – seek.com.au

Recruitment associations

American Staffing Association (ASA) – americanstaffing.net
Recruitment, Consulting and Staffing Association (RCSA) – rcsa.com.au
World Employment Confederation (WEC) – wecglobal.org

Chapter 10

Recruitment, Consulting and Staffing Association (RCSA) – rcsa.com.au
StaffSure – staffsure.org
World Employment Confederation (WEC) – wecglobal.org

Chapter 11

HireVue – hirevue.com
myInterview – myinterview.com
Sonru – modernhire.com/sonru
Spark Hire – sparkhire.com
Vieple – vieple.com

Chapter 14

SalarySiite – salarysiite.com.au

About the author

Erin Devlin GAICD MRCSA is the 2017 RCSA Professional Recruiter of the Year. She leads a team of recruiters as the Managing Director of people2people Recruitment Victoria and has supported thousands of job seekers over the past 14 years. AS CEO of Infront Sports Consulting, she has worked with more than 500 professional athletes and coaches on career transition and planning. She is the Chairman of the VIC/TAS Council for The Recruitment, Consulting & Staffing Association (RCSA), where she works with industry peers to raise professional standards and improve conditions for job seekers, employees and on-hire workers.

Erin studied marketing and human resources at undergraduate level and holds a Graduate Certificate of Business (Dean's List) from Deakin University. She is also a Graduate of the Australian Institute of Company Directors (GAICD), 2012. Erin is a regular commentator on ABC radio, Channel 7, Nine Network, Foxtel, 2UE and Shortlist on careers and employment. She is an engaging speaker, business mentor and recruitment industry leader, passionate about fostering the next generation of talent. She loves helping job seekers secure engaging, meaningful and satisfying employment and set their future up for success.

major st
PUBLISHING

We hope you enjoy reading this book. We'd love you to post a review on social media or your favourite bookseller site. Please include the hashtag #majorstreetpublishing.

Major Street Publishing specialises in business, leadership, personal finance and motivational non-fiction books. If you'd like to receive regular updates about new Major Street books, email info@majorstreet.com.au and ask to be added to our mailing list.

Visit majorstreet.com.au to find out more about our books and authors.

We'd love you to follow us on social media.

- linkedin.com/company/major-street-publishing
- facebook.com/MajorStreetPublishing
- instagram.com/majorstreetpublishing
- @MajorStreetPub

CPSIA information can be obtained
at www.ICGtesting.com
Printed in the USA
LVHW031032260521
688557LV00001B/107